PRAISE FOR

My Heart, the Holy Spirit's Home

My Heart, the Holy Spirit's Home is a heaven-breathed message for this hour. In her practical, down-to-earth style, Lynda beautifully communicates our need for an intimate relationship with the Holy Spirit and the fullness of life that comes as a result. The devotional questions that close each chapter will empower you to challenge anything that is hindering you from embracing an abundant life!

Lisa Bevere
Author and Speaker, Messenger International

Lynda's authenticity and absolute trust in our Redeemer permeates every page of this book. Her words encouraged me to be an even more radical follower of Jesus Christ!

Lisa Harper
Author and Women of Faith Speaker

MY Heart

THE HOLY SPIRIT'S Home

LYNDA HUNTER BJORKLUND

Regal

From Gospel Light
Ventura, California, U.S.A.

Published by Regal
From Gospel Light
Ventura, California, U.S.A.
www.regalbooks.com
Printed in the U.S.A.

© 2011 Lynda Hunter Bjorklund. All rights reserved.
Published in association with the literary agency of Creative Trust, Inc., 5141 Virginia
Way, Suite 320, Brentwood, TN 37027. www.creativetrust.com.

Author photo by Don Jones, P.O. Box 25553, Colorado Springs, CO 80936.

Library of Congress Cataloging-in-Publication Data
Bjorkland, Lynda.
My heart, the Holy Spirit's home : a woman's guide to welcoming the
Holy Spirit into your daily life / Lynda Bjorkland.
p. cm.
ISBN 978-0-8307-5753-4 (trade paper)
1. Christian women—Religious life. 2. Holy Spirit. I. Title. II. Title: Woman's guide
to welcoming the Holy Spirit into your daily life.
BV4527.B58 2011
248.8'43—dc22
2011000052

Rights for publishing this book outside the U.S.A. or in non-English languages
are administered by Gospel Light Worldwide, an international not-for-profit ministry.
For additional information, please visit www.glww.org, email info@glww.org, or write to
Gospel Light Worldwide, 1957 Eastman Avenue, Ventura, CA 93003, U.S.A.

To order copies of this book and other Regal products in bulk quantities,
please contact us at 1-800-446-7735.

Dedication

*I have had the privilege of writing this biography
about a very famous Person. In the process, I've gotten to
know Him even more. This book is dedicated to Him,
the Holy Spirit, and all He's waiting to become
in your life and mine.*

*"My heart is overflowing with a good theme;
I recite my composition concerning the King;
My tongue is the pen of a ready writer."*
PSALM 45:1

Contents

$\mathcal{A}$cknowledgments

*I would like to thank several people who helped to
make this book a reality:*

*Kathy Helmers, who shared the vision.
Kim Bangs, who shared her expertise and excellent eye.
The many women who shared their stories.
And Dave Bjorklund, who shares his life with me.*

Foreword

My Heart, the Holy Spirit's Home gets to the heart of how we can understand the purpose, power and passion of the governor of the Kingdom of Heaven, the Holy Spirit. This is indispensable reading for anyone who wants to understand the Holy Spirit and through Him live life above the norm. It spans the wisdom of the ages, yet breaks new ground in its approach. It will possibly become a classic in this and the next generation.

This erudite, eloquent, and immensely thought-provoking work is one of the most profound, practical and principle-centered approaches to this subject of the Holy Spirit that I have read in a long time. Lynda's approach brings a fresh breath of air that will captivate your heart, engage your mind, and inspire your spirit. She has an amazing ability to leap over complicated theological and metaphysical jargon and reduce complex theories to simple practical principles. She integrates these time-tested precepts about the Holy Spirit into each chapter and gives each a practical application to life, which makes the entire process very user-friendly.

This book will challenge you as it dismantles the mysteries of the Holy Spirit and delivers the profound in simplicity. It will awaken in you the inhibiters that often prevent personal development and empower you to rise above these self-defeating, self-limiting factors and lead to a life of exploits in spiritual and mental advancement. I enjoyed the mind-expanding experience of this exciting book, as every sentence is filled with wisdom. I admonish you to plunge into this ocean of knowledge and watch your life change for the better.

Dr. Myles Munroe, BFM International
ITWLA, Nassau, Bahamas

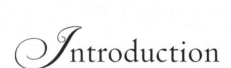

Introduction

As I place my fingers on the keyboard to begin writing this book, I keep remembering a couple of decades-old dreams I have had.

The first dream found me wandering in an unknown location. Desperately, I tried to find my way back, but back to what, I didn't know. I can still recall, however, my sense of lostness, isolation, abandonment and despair.

Then, at last, I stood in a familiar place—behind the Hartfords' house! The Hartfords were an ordinary family who attended the ordinary church my dad pastored in a small, ordinary Indiana town. The church was located nearly 40 backroad miles from our home in Ohio, so our commitment to Wednesday night, Saturday night, Sunday morning and Sunday night services came at a great price. I was the second oldest of what would be eight children, so my mom was either pregnant or nursing much of the 20 years we served at that church.

That's why the possibility of my dream having meaning and coming true scared me to death. I couldn't imagine that God would call me to continue the less-than-glamorous work my parents had begun. After all, I was in my mid-twenties, had recently graduated from college and wanted anything but the ordinary for myself. I still longed to find my "pot of gold" at the end of the rainbow. I still desired to make my mark on the world. Wow, I still wanted to *see* the world!

My second dream was a recurring one. I would observe a special room in a separate section of my house that held exquisite antiques. On rare occasions, I would venture into that extraordinary place to bask in the warmth of what I saw, touched and even smelled. Problem was, I couldn't share the exhilarating experience with many others, as few people appreciated the attraction that I found there. This beauty truly *was* in the eye of the beholder. As a result, I reserved my visits for those who would recognize the value and who would desire to visit that unusual place. When I found them, we would take a walk up the stairs to that sacred room and together share its timeless treasure.

So, why these two dreams? What do they have to do with a book on the Holy Spirit?

Like you, my life today represents the sum of every day I've lived and every event I've experienced. My early days in that Indiana church introduced me to the Holy Spirit. The decades following took me on a circuitous route where I often didn't know my way. But now I find myself returning to that familiar place and looking to the foundational principles I learned then to help me get to where God is taking me now.

And the dream of that special room? That's where you come in. I'm here to share my experience with you. My reacquaintance with the Holy Spirit has sent me into the most beautiful, most alive, most personal, most approachable chapter of my walk with Christ to date. And those who are not interested in seeing this treasure are not reading these words. You are. My guess is that you're one of those special people who recognize the value and desires to go to places you've never been before.

My renewed and enhanced acquaintance with the Holy Spirit has become foundational to everything I do, every day I live, every decision I make, everything I learn from this point forward. And now my goal is to help you do the same. My purpose is to whet *your* appetite for tasting the "something more" through the Holy Spirit. He's the Teacher ready to personalize your individual program of growth in Him. He's the Attendant waiting to take your arm and lead you to places beyond your wildest dreams. He's the Guide who loves to bring the Word alive in your life. He's the real, tangible, hearable part of the Trinity who longs to commune with you throughout your day.

Every time I'm scheduled to speak at a specific location, I receive a request for my "bio." What they're asking me for is information I want others to know about me. In preparing to write this book (my most important book to date, at a most important time), I found myself requesting the same from the Holy Spirit as I prayed, "What do You want *me* to tell *them* about *You?*" This book, *My Heart, the Holy Spirit's Home,* is the result.

After all, mine has been the generation of baby boomers and Holy Spirit busters that somehow managed to misplace the old hymns we used to sing in our churches as well as the stories that moved the writers to pen them. Similarly, we chose to sweep the Holy Spirit under the rug and exchange everything He represents for a more domesticated version of Christianity. In the process, we relinquished our power. I'm determined to do my part in reintroducing Him to the Body of Christ. I want to spend the rest of my days being a spokesperson as well as a do-person—demonstrating all that the Holy Spirit can and will be for us today.

So, come with me. Let's make the trip together up the stairs to that higher place where God has great treasures just waiting to be found.

1

The *Discovery* Begins

And the Spirit of God was hovering over the face of the waters.
GENESIS 1:2

I took my children to Denver one Saturday in December when they were in their early teens. I faced a lot of challenges at the time, including some major issues with one of my children. My heart felt heavy amid the Christmas festivities and decorations that surrounded us.

When we arrived home, I plugged in our Christmas tree, but the lights failed to come on. My son and I worked feverishly on the plug, the bulbs and the cords to fix the problem. Still nothing. It was the last straw, as family members would arrive a couple of days later to celebrate Christmas with us.

Later, I went to bed and cried out to God, describing these difficulties in detail—including my faulty tree lights. Finally, I dried my swollen eyes and fell asleep. That night I dreamed that I pulled off the extension cord from the copy machine, took it to my Christmas tree, connected it at a specific spot and plugged it into the outlet.

At 5:30 the next morning, I awoke and went to my office to spend time with God. While I read my Bible, I remembered the dream and glanced at my copy machine. *Nah!* I thought. But then I changed my mind. What could it hurt?

I did just what I'd seen in my dream, and instantly, my tree was ablaze with white lights. I made myself a bowl of oatmeal while I stood looking out the window at patches of snow in our backyard and thanked God for His help with such a trivial matter. I felt overwhelmed with the fact that because *I* was important to God, my Christmas tree lights were important to Him too.

Then I heard Him speak to my heart, "Consider the lilies." I went to my office and looked up that familiar passage in Matthew 6:25-30 (emphasis added):

> Therefore I say to you, do not worry about your life, what you will eat or what you will drink; nor about your body, what you will put on. Is not life more than food and the body more than clothing? Look at the birds of the air, for they neither sow nor reap nor gather into barns; yet your heavenly Father feeds them. Are you not of more value than they? Which of you by worrying can add one cubit to his stature? So why do you worry about clothing? *Consider the lilies* of the field, how they grow: they neither toil nor spin; and yet I say to you that even Solomon in all his glory was not arrayed like one of these. Now if God so clothes the grass of the field, which today is, and tomorrow is thrown into the oven, will He not much more clothe you, O you of little faith?

As I read those words, I realized that the disciples weren't questioning Jesus *about* the lilies. They were asking Him about what they'd eat and drink—and maybe even about their teenage kids. But Jesus *gave* them the lilies to hold in their hands so they would have faith and keep trusting Him for the things that they couldn't see or feel.

Allow me to stop for a moment and ask you a question. How did you feel as you read this opening vignette?

Skeptical?

Confused?

Out of your comfort zone?

Totally *in* your comfort zone?

Amazed?

Turned off?

Desirous to know more?

I realize that reactions to such an incident run the gamut. Your response depends on your particular teaching, experience and upbringing. You may have witnessed similar events, so mine is completely understandable. Or you may be feeling that if you had had such an experience, you would have attributed it to coincidence or to the taco you ate for dinner the night before. Finally, you may be thinking I'm out in left field and have no clue about what I mean when I say "I had a dream" or "God spoke to my heart." Once, when I published an article in a Christian magazine where I served as editor, a reader wrote to me, asking, "What do you guys have there, a 1-800 number to God? If you do, would you please pass it on?" I'm thinking that you may have already moved to your computer to send me a similar email. But I want you to hear me out.

A February 2010 research study conducted by the Barna Group explored how four different generations of American adults viewed the Holy Spirit. Using a random sample group of 1,005 people age 18 and older, they found that roughly one quarter of all age brackets classified themselves as charismatic (those who claimed to be filled with the Holy Spirit and possessed at least one of the gifts of the Spirit). However, half or more of all respondents saw the Holy Spirit as *present* but not a living entity, including 68 percent of those 18 to 25 years of age.[1] These and other results seemed to indicate that younger Christians are removed from many of the long-standing debates about the Holy Spirit, and so they are more receptive to His roles and functions, but they also seem much less certain about *what* they believe and how to put their faith into action.

That's why solid and freeing and empowering teaching about the Holy Spirit is so necessary: It will help older Christians correct or confirm preconceived beliefs about the Holy Spirit, and younger Christians develop sound theology concerning Him. This book is not a comprehensive treatment *about* the Holy Spirit. It's just the sweet way that I, and other women I have interviewed, have gotten to know Him.

I've discovered that the Holy Spirit living inside us is there to assist us with living life. And the more we use Him, the bigger He stretches. The less we use Him, the more dormant He becomes and the more resigned we get to walking this journey alone—absent of the supernatural.

Just the other day, I had lunch with a friend who looks at me as if I had three eyes when I relate elements of the miraculous. Then I spent time with a friend who is ahead of me in her quest for the deeper manifestations of God. One friend makes me question myself, the other makes me stretch.

The Holy Spirit, and His role and expression in the church and in individual lives, has been a hot-button issue since Jesus went away and left the Kingdom work to us. He has become the proverbial elephant in the church-house room that few talk about, acknowledge or often seek to know in a deeper way.

And yet, Jesus stated that His purpose in leaving was so that He could send the Holy Spirit to dwell in us. The contrast leaves most of us caught somewhere between the charismatic view of the "anything goes" role of the Holy Spirit and the denominational view of "not in my church you won't!"

My goal is to help you bridge the gulf, close the gap and bring together the two parts of you today: first, the religious part that feels that befriending the Holy Spirit could make you fanatical; and second, the desperately hungry part of you that wants something more from your walk of faith and seeks to find that missing power through the Holy Spirit.

Regardless of your life experience, denominational connection or the encouragement you do or do not get from the pulpit, you can know the Holy Spirit in a deeper and more powerful way. It's no accident that you're reading this book. Through both the normal places in life and the difficult times, both personally and corporately, you can have a personal relationship with the One that Jesus went away to make sure you knew—the Holy Spirit. And now is the time to begin that process.

Taking Off the Mask

I grew up watching Saturday morning TV. The lineup included the heroic exploits of a horse named Fury and a dog named Lassie. The morning wasn't complete, however, until I joined in on the adventures of *The Lone Ranger*. I can still hear the music and see the unknown man perched upon his mighty stallion, Silver, balancing valiantly on his back legs. Throughout the 30-minute show, the Lone Ranger galloped about, righting injustices with the aid of his clever Indian sidekick, Tonto, and yelling, "Hi-ho, Silver!" as he rode toward the setting sun.

Problem was, though everyone on the show knew what the Lone Ranger could *do,* no one knew who he *was.* As viewers, we knew the story, so I remember feeling frustrated as people who encountered him continually asked, "Who is that masked man?" The story behind the story was that John Reid was one of six Texas Rangers who were ambushed while chasing a gang of outlaws. After the battle, John Reid was the one "lone ranger" who survived. He was discovered and nursed back to health by Tonto, whose life had been saved by Reid at an earlier time. After he regained his strength, the ranger vowed to hide his identity from the remaining outlaw members and to dedicate his life to making the West a decent place to live. So he donned a black mask to keep his identity a mystery while he accomplished his many feats of justice.

I'm happy to report that the Holy Spirit doesn't wear a mask to disguise Himself, but He *does* involve some mystery that takes our searching to find Him out. He is such a high-value target that He requires diligence and determination from those who want to truly get to know Him. Then He delights in revealing who He really is.

Understanding the Trinity is a good place to begin this revelation. I've heard it described by using the parts of an egg. The shell, yoke and whites are all part of the same egg, yet they are separate and serve different purposes. Others explain the Trinity as the Father being the Executive, the Son being the Architect and the Holy Spirit being the Contractor. However you define the Trinity, certain truths remain:

- They are three parts of one God.
- They are the same in substance, power and glory.
- They work in harmony with one another and operate through the same mind and heart.
- They are three distinct persons and personalities with completely different roles and functions.

The Holy Spirit is the third person of the Trinity. He's the *Spirit* of the Father and Son, and He's divine. The Holy Spirit wasn't an add-on to this trio. He didn't join the Trinity team later in the game. Before time began and there was a God, there was also the Son and the Spirit. All three were present at creation:

- "In the beginning God created the heavens and the earth" (Gen 1:1). God the Father was the planner of creation.

- "And the Spirit of God was hovering [brooding] over the face of the waters" (Gen. 1:2). God the Spirit moved upon and hovered and brooded over all of creation.

- "Then God said, 'Let there be light'; and there was light" (Gen. 1:3). God spoke the Word. And who was that Word? We read in John that Jesus was that Word, the completion of the Trinity: "In the beginning was the Word, and the Word was with God, and the Word was God. He was in the beginning with God. . . . And the Word became flesh and dwelt among us, and we beheld His glory, the glory as of the only begotten of the Father, full of grace and truth" (John 1:1-2,14).

So in the beginning, before anything else was, there was the Trinity: God the Father, God the Word/Jesus being spoken, and God the Holy Spirit. Though the Holy Spirit is equal, He doesn't speak on His own behalf. Instead, He represents the Father and the Son. He's the One who manifests the words that God says. He's the hand of God—His action on earth. He's the transmitter of things from the unseen realm into the seen, natural realm. He's the transformer agent by which the Word became flesh, who then passed on that same Holy Spirit to you and me when He went away.

God in the Flesh

We read nothing about Jesus' life from age 12 until age 30, and He demonstrated none of the *power* of the Godhead until He was baptized with the Holy Spirit. Yes, angels announced at His birth that He was God's Son. But not one of the works that exemplified His ministry—healing, cleansing, casting out of demonic spirits, raising from the dead—became evident until the Holy Spirit came on the scene:

> When He had been baptized, Jesus came up immediately from the water; and behold, the heavens were opened to Him, and He saw the Spirit of God descending like a dove and alighting upon Him. And suddenly a voice came from heaven, saying, "This is My beloved Son, in whom I am well pleased" (Matt. 3:16-17).

Immediately after being anointed with the Holy Spirit, Jesus' ministry was launched. The Spirit led Him into the wilderness, and later Jesus spoke these words in the synagogue:

> The Spirit of the LORD is upon Me, because He has anointed Me to preach the gospel to the poor; He has sent Me to heal the brokenhearted, to proclaim liberty to the captives and recovery of sight to the blind, to set at liberty those who are oppressed; to proclaim the acceptable year of the LORD (Luke 4:18-19).

Jesus' last words before His ascension were instructions to the disciples about the importance of the Holy Spirit in *their* lives. I have to stop here and put on my mother hat as I also step into Jesus' sandals. When my kids were young and I was about to go on a trip, I saved the most important instructions for last. The things

I really needed for them to remember, I spoke to them as I headed out the door. I often reinforced the information with a note left on the kitchen counter and a phone call of reminder.

Jesus did the same as He ended His work here on earth, and the disciples were about to begin theirs. The Son of God turned over His kingdom to the men He had trained, and gave them last-minute instructions to be sure they were up for the task.

What were these important instructions? He told them not to attempt anything until they had been baptized in the Holy Spirit:

> And being assembled together with them, He commanded them not to depart from Jerusalem, but to wait for the Promise of the Father, "which," He said, "you have heard from Me; for John truly baptized with water, but you shall be baptized with the Holy Spirit not many days from now. . . . But you shall receive power when the Holy Spirit has come upon you; and you shall be witnesses to Me in Jerusalem, and in all Judea and Samaria, and to the end of the earth" (Acts 1:4-5,8-9).

Jesus passed on His ministry to the disciples, but instead of telling them to go out and get busy, He told them to wait—wait on the Holy Spirit. They were born again, forgiven, and experienced, but Jesus made it clear that they wouldn't be effective witnesses without the Holy Spirit. Jesus even hung the reason for His departure upon the entrance of the Holy Spirit in their lives and ministries: "Nevertheless I tell you the truth. It is to your advantage that I go away; for if I do not go away, the Helper will not come to you; but if I depart, I will send Him to you" (John 16:7).

So Jesus went away, and the disciples went to work—receiving the Holy Spirit. Though they had seen incredible things take place as they walked alongside Jesus for three years, they had remained pretty dependent and weak. They squabbled about who was the greatest (see Matt. 18:1). They didn't settle His deity in their hearts despite all the miracles they saw (see Matt. 14:22-33). They often failed to mature and grow in their faith (see Matt. 16:21-23). And when Jesus was arrested, they left; one of them even denied—three times—that he knew Jesus (see Matt. 26:69-75).

But *after* they received the Holy Spirit, things radically changed. "When the Day of Pentecost had fully come, they were all with one accord in one place. And suddenly there came a sound from heaven, as of a rushing mighty wind, and it filled the whole house where they were sitting. . . . And they were all filled with the Holy Spirit and began to speak with other tongues, as the Spirit gave them utterance" (Acts 2:1-2,4).

Upon receiving the Holy Spirit, these guys who were weak became strong and bold and brought 3,000 people to Jesus that first day (see Acts 2:41). Three-time-denying Peter and his buddy John performed the first post-Jesus miracle, as they healed the crippled-from-birth man at Gate Beautiful. Peter, filled with the Holy Ghost, went on to confront the men who had crucified Jesus (see Acts 4:8-12).

The salvation Jesus brought saved them, but the Holy Spirit Jesus sent gave them power—power to accomplish the miraculous. And look at some of the results that followed:

- "The Lord added to the church daily those who were being saved" (Acts 2:47).
- "Many of those who heard the word believed; and the number of the men came to be about five thousand" (Acts 4:4).
- "Believers were increasingly added to the Lord, multitudes of both men and women" (Acts 5:14).
- "Then the word of God spread, and the number of disciples multiplied greatly in Jerusalem, and a great many of the priests were obedient to the faith" (Acts 6:7).

Observers who saw the miracles couldn't refute the evidence before them (see 4:14). They couldn't deny what was happening (see 4:16). "They were not able to resist the wisdom and the Spirit by which he [Stephen] spoke" (see 6:10). Everyone went back to their churches and reported what they had seen (see 4:23). As a result, they were of one heart and one soul from denomination to denomination (see 4:32).

All of history had changed, for every person from every walk of faith. The Holy Spirit had arrived on the scene.

Power Comes at a Price

So let's recap. The Holy Spirit has been resident since the beginning. He was the only means by which Jesus could begin and complete His ministry. He was the only means by which the disciples could become productive Kingdom citizens. Jesus went away so that we could have Him.

So where is the Holy Spirit in your church today? Think over the previous month of services you've attended. Where have you observed God's power demonstrated? How many people have you watched being healed or delivered? Who have you seen coming to Christ? Where are you witnessing exponential growth as in those early Acts days because of the miracles that are taking place?

My guess is, most of you found it hard to come up with any answers for the questions posed above. I'm not trying to knock our churches, but I *am* trying to pinpoint what we've lost. Could it be that we've had to come up with a lot of other methods of help because we've abdicated our power?

If we continue with business as usual and keep going to and from church unchanged and unchallenged and unpowered, we will not be ready for what lies ahead. We will also miss opportunities for bringing people to Christ through miracles and demonstrated power. Further, if we fail to assume any of the responsibility for our own growth and that of our churches, our lifetimes won't reflect a fraction of the victory and amazing experiences the Holy Spirit is waiting to provide.

You and I need more than a sedentary relationship with God. We've got to get out and move around with the Holy Spirit. We need to exercise our gifts and callings and passions in Him. That takes place in our individual workout sessions with the Holy Spirit, in those daily quiet places. He's your personal trainer. That means He needs to meet with you every day to direct your workout needs and to address the problem and identify the growth areas required in your life.

Through the years, I've seen churches and faith experience *with* the power of the Holy Spirit, and I've see it *without*. I've observed powerful moves of God where the Holy Spirit is allowed to operate without restraint; and I've seen the neutered, emasculated, bound-up, boxed-in powerless version of the Holy Spirit and the ways the Body of Christ attempts to compensate for that loss.

Sure, mistakes are made as we press in to a deeper place and understanding of the Holy Spirit. The Bible tells us that when there are no oxen in the barn, the stalls stay clean, but where the oxen are, messes result (see Prov. 14:4). The Christian world as a whole tends to be far more forgiving to those churches and individuals within them who aren't even trying to go further or access the present-day power of the Holy Spirit. They seem to recognize, provide accolades to and sign up for those places where the stalls are clean. I'd rather see a few messes where God is moving than no mess where we've become content with the status quo.

I urge you, don't throw the baby out with the bath water. Don't let the messes prevent you from finding the prize that is waiting on the other side—a rich and abundant and vibrant and living relationship with the Holy Spirit that will last the rest of your days.

Think You Might Want to Know More?

Recently, I watched a Christian TV program. A well-known singer was conducting interviews with the people on the set. I looked at the singer, remembering my acquaintance with him. I knew him well in some of my earlier work. As I watched his talent on display, I felt proud that I knew him. But even more, he knew me. Mention my name, and he would probably talk to you about some of the times we'd had together, some of the qualities he knew best about me.

Later that day, I went hiking. I was still thinking about the singer I had seen. Suddenly, I was no longer thinking about *him*, but about *Him*—the Holy Spirit. I not only know Him, but He knows me!

And the coolest part of it all is that He is not a duplicate. The *same* spirit that hovered over the face of the waters before the world was ever created speaks to me today to pray for someone. The *same* Spirit that raised Jesus from the dead lives in me (see Rom. 8:11) and helped me light my Christmas tree lights that morning. I could feel His presence in my kitchen while I baked cookies for our home fellowship. I sensed His pleasure as I sang songs of praise.

Every day of my life, the yearning grows stronger. "My soul longs, yes even faints for the courts of the LORD; My heart and my flesh cry out for the living God" (Ps. 84:2). I don't just want to know *about* Him. I don't just want to read about what others are discovering about Him. I want to pull back the curtain and discover God's Spirit as I would get to know a cherished friend. And then I want to pass it on.

He rewards those who diligently seek Him (see Heb. 11:6), and He's excited to take off the mask that religion has placed on Him. I recently attended a conference in California, where the supernatural has become normal. The Holy Spirit was evident in everything they were accomplishing there. After three days of witnessing the most amazing events, I glanced in my rearview mirror as I pulled away from that city and headed toward the airport. I smiled and thanked my Lord that I was not leaving Him behind with those wonderful friends in Christ. Instead, the Holy Spirit was right there with me, too, and together we were headed in the same direction.

The Holy Spirit is everywhere at work and looking for those who will get to work with Him. For some time now, one of my passionate prayers has become, "God, make it mine." I read lots of books and Bible stories about ways the Holy Spirit assumed regular roles in other people's lives. I hear testimonies about how the Holy Spirit has shown up in real time for real situations for real human beings. But I want to personalize it. I've been praying that He would "make it mine," so that I might uncover everything He has ever wanted to create *in* me, and every reality He has desired to become *to* me.

And now my prayer has expanded to, "Make it yours." I pray that you will take every truth I present in this book and make it yours—apply it to your specific life and use it as a starting point for your exciting adventure with the Holy Spirit. All you have to do is ask Him, and begin the process. He'll take it from there.

Before you know it, you will realize that the Holy Spirit is, indeed, at home in your heart. And that is just the place you want Him to be.

---

*M*ake It Yours
Begin Your Discovery

You've already seen how the Trinity was present from the start of the Old Testament. Now take a look at where the Trinity turned up in the New Testament. The Great Commission is one such place:

> And Jesus came and spoke to them, saying, "All authority has been given to Me in heaven and on earth. Go therefore and make disciples of all the nations, baptizing them in the name of the Father and of the Son and of the Holy Spirit, teaching them to observe all things that I have commanded you; and lo, I am with you always, even to the end of the age" (Matt. 28:18-20).

The word "authority" used here is the Greek word *exousia* (which we will talk more about in chapter 7). Briefly, it means "delegated liberty to exercise the full power of attorney in all God's interests." It means "complete authority to act in God's stead as if God Himself were doing the work."

Write out Matthew 9:8 below, an important verse containing the word *exousia*:

_____

_____

_____

_____

Jesus' power was unlimited in doing the will and works of God on earth. Read the following verses that show that unlimited power:

- Matthew 4:23-24
- Matthew 8:17
- Matthew 10:1-8
- Mark 1:27
- Luke 4:36
- Luke 10:19
- John 5:27
- John 17:2

Then Jesus received all power in heaven and in earth. Read these verses that demonstrate that power:

- Ephesians 1:20-23
- Colossians 2:9-17
- Hebrews 1:3
- Hebrews 7:25
- 1 Peter 3:22

Then Jesus promised to share His earthly power with His followers. Take a look at these important verses that pull you into the equation:

- Matthew 16:19
- Matthew 18:18

Then came the Great Commission. Before Jesus went away, He passed the baton of authority to His followers. Jesus is saying, "In view of My authority, I commission you with full power of attorney (legal authority to transact business for another) to carry on the work that I have started." And then the Trinity comes in: "Go therefore and make disciples of all the nations, baptizing them in the name of the Father and of the Son and of the Holy Spirit, teaching them to observe all things that I have commanded you;

and lo, I am with you always, even to the end of the age" (Matt. 28:19). Your legal authority carries with it the force of all three members of the Godhead—not by the authority of Jesus only.

So what does this mean in real life? Think about the biggest problem area you are dealing with right now. Make it one that holds no earthly solution. Now insert the details of that problem into the prayer confession below.

PRAYER CONFESSION

Holy Spirit, thank You for the Word. Thank You that You are beginning a new process in me. Thank You that You are becoming real to me. And thank You that in Jesus' name, I possess the keys of the kingdom of heaven. Whatever I bind on earth will be bound in heaven, and whatever I loose on earth will be loosed in heaven. That includes

_____

_____

_____

_____

The best part of it all is that now that I realize that truth and invoke the name of Jesus for my situation, all three of You show up to back me. I'm not speaking on my own but through the inherited and delegated authority that You all give me. Let me never forget that for the rest of my days. As soon as I speak the words in faith, let me picture with my spiritual eyes the Father, Son and Holy Spirit standing right there behind me. Thank You. Amen.

Note

1. Adrienne S. Gaines, "Study Shows Charismatic Generation Gap," *Charisma*, March 29, 2010. http://www.charismamag.com/index.php/news/26647-new-study-shows-pentecostal-generation-gap.

2

His Story

And suddenly there came a sound from heaven, as of a rushing mighty wind, and it filled the whole house where they were sitting.
ACTS 2:2

My husband, Dave, grew up and spent most of his adult life in Minnesota, so we find ourselves visiting there often. Recently, St. Paul featured an amazing Titanic exhibit at the Science Museum of Minnesota Omnitheater. Visitors were drawn to 1912 upon entrance as each received a boarding pass of an actual passenger. Then they began a journey through the life of the Titanic—from its construction to what it offered onboard to its ill-fated sinking. Hundreds of authentic artifacts and extensive room re-creations of the ship were on display: perfume from a maker who sold his samples, china etched with the logo of the elite White Star Line, and even a 300-pound portion of the Titanic's hull were among the objects that observers could see.

Equally amazing as the incredible artifacts was the setting in which they were located. The omnitheater holds 375 people who can look up, down, right, and left and find themselves fully surrounded by the crystal-clear visual and audio components. A convertible dome screen moves overhead like a sunroof on a car. Through this remarkable technology, visitors left with a comprehensive and chronological understanding of the history of the Titanic.

Every once in a while, God gives us the privilege of a similar experience. Examining the Holy Spirit's story from the beginning until now is one such time. I've always been a visual, big-picture, big-screen person. So when I'm permitted to observe things from God's perspective, the large aerial view actually becomes smaller, manageable and embraceable. The exercise reminds me that there *is* a method in the madness of life, a plan in the seeming pandemonium. It gives me a glimpse of where we've come from and where we're going. God holds the blueprints of His project in the palm of His hand. And I come away, once again, remembering that He knows the end from the beginning: "Declaring the end from the beginning, and from ancient times the things that are not yet done, saying, 'My counsel shall stand, and I will do all my pleasure'" (Isa. 46:10).

Like the Titanic display, we can look up, down, right, and left and find ourselves fully surrounded by the crystal-clear display of God's movement since day one—the unfolding of His master plan as He does His pleasure. Examining these truths in this way stills us and allows God to be God (see Ps. 46:10). By doing that now, we can begin a journey through the life of the Holy Spirit—His presence at the beginning, middle and end of mankind. After all, the Holy Spirit's presence spans the first chapter of Scripture—"And the Spirit of God was hovering over the face of the waters" (Gen. 1:2)—to the last chapter of Scripture—"And the Spirit and the bride say, 'Come!' And let him who hears say, 'Come!' And let him who thirsts come" (Rev. 22:17).

So sit back and be amazed through the original omnitheater revelation of God's Word. Observe, understand and realize the heritage that is yours—through the Holy Spirit.

Scene One: The Creation

First, God ruled only over the invisible, heavenly world. Then He created a visible, physical world to enlarge His domain, which He called earth. Then He made man with a physical body to rule over His new physical world.

God said, "Let Us make man in Our image, according to Our likeness; let them have dominion over the fish of the sea, over the birds of the air, and over the cattle, over all the earth and over every creeping thing that creeps on the earth." So God created man in His own image; in the image of God He created him; male and female He created them (Gen. 1:26-27).

And He breathed His own Spirit into that man to give him power for fulfilling His work in that physical world. "And the LORD God formed man of the dust of the ground, and breathed into his nostrils the breath of life; and man became a living being" (Gen. 2:7). This "living being" came alive in three ways:

1. His *spirit* was created to be like God's.
2. His *soul* contained his mind, will and emotions and allowed him to communicate with God
3. His *body* became the house for God's Spirit and man's soul.

When God breathed His Spirit into man, He moved inside. Think about that. God decided to set up His earthly throne within man. He would govern the physical world from there. He would also convene on man all Kingdom rights, dominion and authority over everything on the earth. Through His Spirit, God and man would openly communicate, and man would receive all the power he would need to perform his work.

Man's *assignment* was to bring about the policies from the invisible world into the visible world. Man's *goal* was to make the earthly kingdom look like the heavenly Kingdom. And God's Spirit was the key to it all. He became the connection of earth to heaven through man.

Scene Two: The Fall

But then Lucifer instigated a ruckus in heaven that ultimately affected earth. This former angel led a rebellion to replace God's authority with man's. Adam and Even caught the rebellion bug and ate from the forbidden tree. God drove them from the Garden (see Gen. 3:24) because man was no longer equipped with God's nature to live there. They had forfeited their purity and holiness. It cost them not only their home in the Kingdom, but also God recalled His Spirit. Adam and Eve had separated themselves—and all humanity to follow—from God, His Spirit and His heavenly Kingdom.

This caused mankind to begin living life from the outside in instead of from the inside out. They'd had the edge when the Holy Spirit was resident within. But that was gone. The outside world now provided only what their physical senses told them. "Then the eyes of both of them were opened, and they knew that they were naked; and they sewed fig leaves together and made themselves coverings" (Gen. 3:7).

The consequences? Man's body now took over where the Spirit had ruled before. Our spiritual perspective had become a sensual one. We lost our power. We forgot heavenly values and instituted new ones in their place. Evil spread. Chaos ensued.

But just as soon as the Fall happened, the God who loved humanity came back on the scene and promised the Spirit's return and a new earthly kingdom that would mirror the heavenly one. This fresh hope would come through God's Son who would be born on earth. He would restore the Kingdom and man's power and authority to rule there. And He would do it all through the return of the Holy Spirit—the central reason for the whole restoration process.

All the stories found in the Old Testament lead up to the eventual restoration of God's Spirit to men so they could rule and reign. The Holy Spirit would once again connect the earth to heaven. The Holy Spirit would once again live on the inside of man.

Scene Three: The Unfolding

But between the Fall and the fulfillment of the promised Son, God's plan to completely reinstate the Holy Spirit came about in stages. God's Plan A was behind, and Plan B lay just ahead.

I want to briefly pause here before I go on to explain the rest of what I'm calling Plan B. The Fall didn't surprise God, and it didn't leave Him scrambling and wondering what to do. He didn't hurriedly reconfigure the Holy Spirit's assignment on earth nor randomly pick the country of Israel—nor do anything else that was not precisely a part of His itinerary for humanity. The same God whom I described earlier as holding the master plan in His hand is the same God who instituted everything that we're talking about here. What I am calling Plan B is actually the expanded version of Plan A, though as humans we find it difficult to completely understand how this can be so. But it is.

So what was included in that Plan B?

The Holy Spirit Made Occasional Appearances

Instead of living inside of man, the Holy Spirit now came briefly "upon" certain individuals after the Fall to accomplish supernatural tasks. It was like a temporary empowerment granted for the glory of God that equipped the receivers to do something they could not ordinarily do. Observers who lived after Eden but before the Kingdom got a glimpse of God and a harbinger of what would be again some day. The Spirit of the Lord came *upon* Saul, and he prophesied. It turned him into another man (see 1 Sam. 10:6). The Spirit of the Lord came *upon* Samson, and he tore lions apart (see Judg. 14:6). These and countless other examples happened because the "upon" experience came to make the difference in those days.

God Showcased Israel

God also picked a tiny nation to illustrate what He had always had in mind for mankind as a whole. Israel would not benefit exclusively from God's love but would become the example of what God had to offer all. This microcosm called Israel would be the visual reminder for all generations of the favor of God on His chosen people. The Israelites sometimes did well in their example to the world, but more often than not, they messed up. God's mercy, however, threaded its way throughout the nation's story, and so throughout ours.

And the same God who has it all figured out is the same God who provided for His people before the Fall as well as after. His provision has always been there for those He loves, though His techniques of delivery would vary in the generations to come. Let's go on to discover how.

God Used Priests

God brought Israel out of their subservience in Egypt and invited them to become a nation of priests (see Exod. 19:6) with personal access to Him. But the Israelites said to Moses, "You speak with us, and we will hear; but let not God speak with us, lest we die" (Exod. 20:19). The Israelites chose to have a mediator instead of accepting God's offer to come to them directly. They chose the law instead of grace. Scripture would later tell us that the law came from Moses but grace would come through Jesus (see John 1:17).

So God appointed priests from Israel's tribe of Levi to become mediators for His people. They went into the Holy of Holies and interceded on behalf of the people. A provision God instituted for that time was something called the Urim and Thummim. These words mean "light and complete truth." They were some type of device (perhaps a stone) that was used to determine messages from God for specific situations. God told Moses to put this provision in the priest's breastplate (see Exod. 28:30) so the priest could ascertain answers for the people. Then when the sinless high priest went into the Holy of Holies and offered a sacrifice for the Israelites, the Spirit of God came and dwelt temporarily between the cherubim and mercy seat within the holiness He found there.

The arrangement for mediators worked out okay until the priests became corrupt and were no longer holy. As happened at the Fall, God's Spirit could not remain where sin existed. By the time priest Eli's sons (see 1 Sam. 2:22-25) and priest Samuel's sons (see 1 Sam. 8:2-3) cranked up the evil level several notches in their own work, once again, God recalled His Spirit and ended His mediation through the priests. So God instituted another provision.

God Used Kings

The invisible Creator God wasn't enough for the Israelites. They wanted a ruler with skin on, so they clamored for a king: "Now make us a king to judge us like all the nations" (1 Sam. 8:5). As we saw earlier, God's original design for mankind included that they would all rule, reign and exercise dominion over the whole earth (see Gen. 1:26-27). Rulers, reigners and dominion-takers don't require kings, but those who settle for less do. The people continued to beg for a king (see 1 Sam. 8:7), so just as God sent meat when they demanded it for dinner instead of His perfect manna, God gave them kings. Saul, then David, then a lineup of mostly unremarkable rulers came on the scene, only a few of whom reigned in godly ways. The day would ultimately come when God would send the King of kings and allow us to co-rule with Him. But until then, human kings had to do.

God Used Prophets

In the absence of holy priests and kings, God sent prophets to speak on His behalf and to try to reconnect the people with the heavenly realm. Not only were priests and kings no longer part of God's provision for this time, but the Urim and Thummim also disappeared. The prophets had taken their place, and this provision played out with ordinary human beings.

For example, in 2 Kings 4:8-37 we see that whenever the prophet Elisha and his servant went through the town of Shunem, they stayed with a well-to-do couple who'd made an apartment for them above their garage. One day, Elisha asked the woman what he could do to repay their kindness.

Both the husband and wife were players in this story, but it is the wife that Elisha interacted with. This barren woman asked for a son. So Elisha prayed, and God answered. However, trouble happened one day when their probably teenaged son was working in the field with his father. He grabbed his head in pain, and his father instructed the servants to take him to his mother. The son died.

Instead of becoming bitter or angry that the gift she had been given had been taken away, she demonstrated faith in God's provision for that day. She laid her dead son on Elisha's bed, had her husband saddle a donkey, and headed out to search for "the man of God" (2 Kings 4:22). Once she found him, Elisha's servant asked, "Is everything okay?"

"Oh, yes," she replied. "All is well."

"How about your husband and your son?" the servant asked.

"All is well," she said. Then she went to Elisha. "Oh, by the way. My son is dead. Would you come and help us out?"

Elisha did, God did, and the son was alive again.

What an amazing story! God helped *that* woman for *that* problem for *that* time. But the woman's response was also amazing. She knew that all was well even when evidence appeared to the contrary. She had utter and complete confidence—her knowledge down deep inside—that God's provision through the prophet would be sufficient. Even in the face of death, she continued to trust—and God came through.

More needs were met as more prophets followed—and all of them continued to point to the One who was to come.

Scene Four: The Son Shines

Several hundred years later, the angel Gabriel was sent by God to a city of Galilee called Nazareth. The angel told Mary, "The Holy Spirit will come upon you, and the power of the Highest will overshadow you; therefore, also, that Holy One who is to be born will be called the Son of God" (Luke 1:35).

What had happened? The Holy Spirit was back. He had returned to dwell within the sinless person of Jesus Christ until the rest of humanity could accept Him too.

As we discussed in chapter 1, John baptized Jesus in the Jordan River: "And the Holy Spirit descended in bodily form like a dove upon Him. . . . Then Jesus, being filled with the Holy Spirit, returned from the Jordan and was led by the Spirit into the wilderness" (Luke 3:22; 4:1). First, Jesus was *born* of the Spirit (see Luke 1:35). Then He was *filled* with the Spirit. Only then could He begin His ministry and *deliver* the Holy Spirit to the people on earth.[1]

The One whom John had announced to bring the Holy Spirit had come: "John answered, saying to all, 'I indeed baptize you with water, but One mightier than I is coming, whose sandal strap I am not worthy to loose. He will baptize you with the Holy Spirit and with fire'" (Luke 3:16).

So Jesus became the provision for the next three years. "God, who at various times and in various ways spoke in time past to the fathers by the prophets, has in these last days spoken to us by His Son" (Heb. 1:1-2). He walked from place to place healing the sick, raising the dead, delivering the oppressed and bringing people to Himself.

Take the day that Jesus came to a town called Nain, a neighboring city of Shunem, where nearly 900 years before, the prophet Elisha had raised the woman's son from the dead. This time, the provision was Jesus, and He came upon the funeral of another dead son of another sad woman. And like the prophet before, Jesus touched the deceased and he came back to life (see Luke 7:11-15).

Yes, Jesus was the provision for that day. But He only reached those He came in contact with. So the final provision had to be made. Jesus' suffering, His death and His resurrection from the dead became the means to the final, glorious end.

Scene Five: The Baptism *in* the Holy Spirit

The whole reason for Jesus coming to earth was to break Satan's stronghold, destroy rebellion's control and reconnect mankind to God through the Holy Spirit. It's what made God's redemptive process necessary (see John 16:7).

When Jesus died on the cross, the temple veil was ripped from top to bottom (see Matt. 27:51), signifying that the Holy Spirit was back as it had been between the cherubim and mercy seat in the Holy of Holies. This act let the Holy Spirit out and allowed us to go in. The third Person of the Trinity had found a holy place to dwell once again. Then Pentecost happened: "And suddenly there came a sound from heaven, as of a rushing mighty wind, and it filled the whole house where they were sitting. . . . And they were all filled with the Holy Spirit and began to speak with other tongues, as the Spirit gave them utterance" (Acts 2:2,4).

The Holy Spirit had arrived along with His power, and the disciples went on to flip the world upside down (see Acts 17:6).

We've Become Part of the Narrative

The story of the Holy Spirit has a much better ending than does the story of the Titanic. Following man's mess-up, resulting in the loss of the Holy Spirit, God promised His return. It's the most important promise heaven ever made to earth, and it's the key to every person's search for life's meaning.

If one thing is clear from this panoramic view, it's that God redeems. Redemption is pregnant with hope and newness and life instead of death. Through the years, I have taken worthless ground and made it into a beautiful garden. I have pulled leftovers from my refrigerator and made them into a delicious soup. I have salvaged old pieces of furniture and made them centerpieces in a room. All were left to be discarded, but all were redeemed.

Redemption means "making good" or "making right." It means "rebirth, reclamation, reparation, restitution, retrieval, rescue and renewal." All good; all redemption. And redemption is ours. God gave humanity one chance, and we blew it. So He gave us another and another and another. But He held out on His Spirit until we could reclaim holiness. While God is abundant in mercy, He cannot dwell where there is sin. So He sent His Son to remove our sin and to make way for His Spirit's return. And that Spirit would accomplish what Jesus Himself could not do without the Spirit—dwell inside every believer and do whatever we need for Him to do through us (see John 14:16-26; 16:15-17).

I heard a story once of a man who visited Iran and watched rug makers weave exquisite Persian rugs. He said their technique involved the workers forming a circle around the master weaver who sat in the middle. The observer asked one of the workers, "What do you do when you make a mistake? Do you start over? Do you throw it away?"

The worker told the man that when he made a mistake, he carried his creation to the master weaver who examined and carefully studied what he'd done. Then the master weaver painstakingly redesigned the pattern so that it incorporated the mistake, and he handed it back for the worker to carry on.

Mankind made a big mistake, but immediately the Master Weaver studied and released His new plan of redemption that incorporated our mistakes. That plan ultimately brought back what He'd planned all along: God's presence; God's reconnection of man with heaven; God's Spirit.

Make It Yours
Understand His Story

Based on what you've read in this chapter, write a brief description of the Holy Spirit's history. For each era, what did He do, and how did He manifest Himself?

Scene One

_____

_____

_____

Scene Two

_____

_____

_____

Scene Three

_____

_____

_____

Scene Four

_____

_____

_____

Scene Five

_____

_____

_____

Throughout Scripture, the dove symbolizes gentleness, innocence and meekness, and it was offered in sacrifice (see Lev. 12:6; 14:22)—especially for the poor who could not afford a lamb (see Lev. 12:8). Jesus' family brought two small doves in place of a lamb for a sacrifice (see Luke 2:24). The dove serves another role in the Bible: it is a type or shadow of the Holy Spirit. The term is used to describe what the Holy Spirit might be like:

> And Jesus, when he was baptized, went up straightway out of the water: and, lo, the heavens were opened unto him, and he saw the Spirit of God descending like a *dove*, and lighting upon him (Matt. 3:16, *KJV,* emphasis added).

Write out the following two other passages that refer to this event and any additional details you observe:

Mark 1:9-11

_____

_____

_____

Luke 3:21-22

_____

_____

_____

What was the purpose of the Holy Spirit's anointing on Jesus?

_____

_____

_____

_____

As we have already noted, Jesus went from this experience through 40 days in the wilderness and on to do the work He had been sent to do. The Holy Spirit's lighting like a dove presents a picture of the character and manner of Jesus' redemptive ministry through both gentleness and sacrifice. Now read the following account in Genesis 8:8-12 of Noah as he tries to determine when the waters of the flood had receded enough for him to exit the ark:

> He [Noah] also sent out from himself a dove, to see if the waters had receded from the face of the ground. But the dove found no resting place for the sole of her foot, and she returned into the ark to him, for the waters were on the face of the whole earth. So he put out his hand and took her, and drew her into the ark to himself. And he waited yet another seven days, and again he sent the dove out from the ark. Then the dove came to him in the evening, and behold, a freshly plucked olive leaf was in her mouth; and Noah knew that the waters had receded from the earth. So he waited yet another seven days and sent out the dove, which did not return again to him anymore.

Remember that the dove represents the Holy Spirit. Many Bible scholars see these references to a dove in Genesis 8:8-12 as types or shadows of the three distinct Holy Spirit "dispensations." A dispensation is defined as an "arrangement or plan." We might see it as a "role." The Genesis story provides a different but similar way of looking at the various "scenes" we examined in chapter 2, illustrating the arrangements, plans or roles of the Holy Spirit throughout time. The three dispensations depicted in this passage are: (1) Old Testament dispensation (Genesis through Malachi);

(2) Gospel dispensation (Matthew through John); and (3) Church-age dispensation (Day of Pentecost through today).

Old Testament Dispensation. "But the dove found no resting place for the sole of her foot, and she returned into the ark to him, for the waters were on the face of the whole earth. So he put out his hand and took her, and drew her into the ark to himself" (Gen. 8:8-9). The dove was sent out but found no place to rest, so it returned. This represented the way the Holy Spirit ministered during the age of the Old Testament. Sin entered at the Fall, so the Holy Spirit, who had hovered since the beginning, had to leave. Throughout the Old Testament generations that followed, the Holy Spirit only came *upon* individuals so they could accomplish specific, humanly impossible tasks. Then, immediately upon completion of the job, that same Holy Spirit departed.

Describe how this act is apparent in the following passages:

1 Samuel 10:6,10

_____

_____

_____

1 Samuel 11:6

_____

_____

_____

1 Samuel 6:14

_____

_____

_____

Judges 13:25

_____

_____

_____

Judges 14:6,19

_____

_____

_____

Judges 15:14

_____

_____

_____

Judges 16:19

_____

_____

_____

Under the Old Covenant dispensation, the Spirit found no place to light or remain. God dealt with people through all they had—their soul/flesh/physical realm. He couldn't work through their spirits because they were spiritually dead, separated from God. He's the *Holy* Spirit, and He cannot live where unholiness exists. Under the Old Testament covenant, people had no way of purging their unholiness. As a result, God lived in the Holy of Holies, and the tabernacle rituals replaced God's personal communication with man.

Unfortunately, many Christians still practice Old Testament dispensation. They act as if God, through His Spirit and His anointing, comes and goes. David prayed, "Create in me a clean heart, O God, and renew a steadfast spirit within me" (Ps. 51:10), but he lived under the Old Covenant, wasn't born again and didn't have God's Spirit *in* him. It's not the same for us, as we will see.

Gospel dispensation. "Then the dove came to him in the evening, and behold, a freshly plucked olive leaf was in her mouth; and Noah knew that the waters had receded from the earth" (Gen. 8:11). The dove was sent out and returned with a leaf, a sign of peace. This signified the end of the judgment era and the beginning of the working of the Holy Spirit in a particular way during the Gospels through the person of Jesus Christ, the *Prince* of Peace.

Jesus spent His ministry preparing a way for God to come and dwell in people as He did in the beginning. But something had to happen to make us holy enough for God's Spirit to dwell in us, so Jesus died on the cross; and when He did, judgment of the earth was finished. Sin had been dealt with once and for all. Iniquity that had only been covered up in the Old Testament, and so required a regular sacrifice, had now been removed. With sin dealt with and holiness at last achievable, the earth was prepared for the fullness of the Holy Spirit.

How did the life, death and resurrection of Jesus Christ affect you personally?

_____

_____

_____

What new opportunities did Jesus' sacrifice present for you?

_____

_____

_____

Church-age dispensation. "So he waited yet another seven days and sent out the dove, which did not return again to him anymore" (Gen. 8:12). The dove was sent out and didn't return. He had found a place to light and remain. Jesus had become the perfect sacrifice who paid the price for us all. By faith, all we had to do was accept that sacrifice and be born again. And the Holy Spirit had a holy place where He could at last set up permanent residence (see John 14:16).

The Holy Spirit would abide forever, not come and go as He did under the Old Covenant. We're back to being what He created us to be—His dwelling place on planet earth. So wherever we go, the Holy Spirit shows up. Even when we don't feel Him, He is still there. We don't have to beg or sing Him into coming. Instead, we can raise our voices in praise and acknowledgment of His presence. The Holy Spirit is there sitting or standing or lying right where you are. That's something to raise your voice about! And it kind of makes you think more about what you say and watch and think, doesn't it?

Write out and memorize the following verses, which will remind you of this permanent live-in condition of the Holy Spirit inside you:

Matthew 28:20

_____

_____

_____

_____

Hebrews 13:5b

_____

_____

_____

_____

Romans 8:35-39

_____

_____

_____

Given the information you have learned about the Holy Spirit, if you could choose a time period in which to live, would it be?

- The Old Testament dispensation, where the Holy Spirit could fall temporarily on you so you could do a mighty act?

- The Gospel dispensation, where you could actually see and walk with Jesus?

- Or the Church-age dispensation, where the Holy Spirit comes to live inside you from the moment you are born again and will never leave you?

Why would you choose this specific time period?

_____

_____

_____

_____

_____

PRAYER CONFESSION

Holy Spirit, thank You that when I went to sleep last night, You stayed awake. Thank You that when I awoke this morning, I didn't have to cry and beg You to come back. You are with me all the time in Your fullness. Thank You that I live in this day and time when the earth is full of the knowledge of the Lord as the waters cover the sea (see Hab. 2:14). How? By Your people demonstrating Your glory, the manifest presence of God. When people see me, I want them to see You. Thank You that I am conformed to the image of Jesus (see Rom. 8:29), the express image of God. Thank You that You will never, ever leave me. Amen.

Note

1. A major theme of the New Testament is that Jesus did not do miracles by virtue of His divine nature but through His total dependence on the Holy Spirit. In Philippians 2:6-7, Paul makes it clear that Jesus emptied Himself of His divine powers when He came to earth. Luke 4:1 and 14 state that Jesus was filled with and empowered by the Holy Spirit *before* He started His earthly ministry of healing and miracles, and the Gospel of John notes that Jesus was completely dependent on the Father (obviously through the Holy Spirit) in all that He did and said during His ministry (see John 3:34; 5:19; 7:16; 8:28; 12:49-50; 14:10).

 My Story

Your ears shall hear a word behind you, saying, "This is the way, walk in it,"
Whenever you turn to the right hand or whenever you turn to the left.
ISAIAH 30:21

The story of the Hunter family's spiritual journey began in 1952, when I was six months old. Neither of my parents were Christians, and my mother said she had never heard "God" mentioned while she was growing up. But then doctors gave her 18-year-old sister, Joan, with a rheumatic heart, a fatal diagnosis. An early Christmas and graduation followed.

Then one dog-day summer afternoon, my grandpa heard of a man who had come to Hamilton, Ohio, to hold revivals. Grandpa found himself fresh out of options, so he suggested taking Joan for prayer. My mother opposed, saying, "Over my dead body will you take her there," and the doctor told him that moving Joan could mean certain death.

Despite the opposition, Grandpa headed to that tent revival with his dying daughter, her pounding heart visible through the tent dress she wore to cover her swollen body. I can almost see my grandfather, who owned a sawmill, in his dark-green work clothes and heavy boots crunching the grass beneath as he made his way to the front of that tent while disregarding protocol. But the preacher prayed for Joan that Friday night, and by Tuesday, she was completely healed. She lived to see another 55 Christmases and many grandchildren and great-grandchildren in the years to come.

Jumping in with Both Feet

That's how my parents were introduced to Christ. They not only got to know God, but they also saw a demonstration of His power. The works of God had been revealed to them (see John 9:3). As a result, they found it impossible to walk back from that experience. The only way they saw was forward. They immediately turned their lives over to Christ, learning as they went along and pressing into the miraculous. My mother said, "I had to know this Lord who would heal my little sister."

And know Him she did. I would hear her praying in our pantry/furnace room. I would see her red eyes and streaked face following one of her passionate encounters with God. I would watch her devour the Bible and share what she had learned whenever she could steal a precious moment.

As a result, the miraculous became a common event in the Hunter home. My brother Phill mashed his finger one afternoon in the front door and watched a bone topple to the porch floor. Mom did the only thing she knew—she prayed. Then she picked up the bone, placed it back on his finger and bandaged it. Within a few days, not even a scar remained. Today, we don't remember which finger was involved.

I saw similar results played out when my family faced countless other illnesses, financial challenges and difficult situations. In all of those situations, we went to God. It's what we'd learned to do, and it's what we did. We also became part of a bigger body of believers. Mom and Dad helped to build The Lighthouse Gospel Tabernacle in Metamora, Indiana, a small church in an impoverished area of the state. In later years, Dad became the pastor in addition to his work as a postman.

As for Me . . .

I observed much of my parents' floundering after they'd jumped in the deep end and started learning to spiritually swim. I also benefited from the miracles and sound health that resulted from their intense reliance on God. Tongues, prophecies and healings were regular occurrences in our services. I realized these things were weird to other people, but their validity was more important to me at that time than whether or not someone thought we were strange. I saw people healed and accidents averted. I heard words of wisdom spoken to people by prophets who had no way of knowing such details. And when I played the piano and someone began to "give a prophecy," I knew to stop playing in reverence until the interpretation came.

Sure, I saw some things done unwisely, but I also saw them done well and effectively, often in life-changing ways. It's because of what I saw done right that I became convinced in my heart that these things were real and that God could be something more than a name in a Bible or a sermon from the pulpit. He could be personal and applicable to real issues. That's the God I decided I wanted—especially based on my mother's example—even though it would be many years before I surrendered my own life to Him instead of relying on my parents' faith.

And then there was the dichotomous way we lived. Our Ohio home was in a university town where going to college was the norm. Meanwhile, we attended church several times each week among rare high school graduates, some even dropping out by age 14. Like skiing down a mountainside, I often felt as if we traversed two totally different worlds. One was more socially acceptable but devoid of anything spiritual. The other became a source of ridicule by many but offered a greater hope and comfort for our growing family.

As I became a teenager interested in boys, I found the pickin's slim at our church. Because of our Indiana commitments, I wasn't able to get involved with normal high school activities. Then came college, which for me was a continuation of high school. I lived at home and worked at three jobs to get an elementary education degree from the university in our town. (I only knew of two choices in those days for women to major in—nursing or teaching—and I couldn't stand the sight of blood, so teaching became my career of default.) When I was about 20, I turned my back on much of my spiritual foundation and focused, instead, on other things. At age

21, I became the first college graduate in the history of my family. My life had taken off but without God leading the way.

Life Decisions

After getting my master's degree and teaching for several years, I got married at age 27. I married a nonbeliever, but because my life was not where it needed to be either, it didn't seem that important at the time. However, six years later, when I was pregnant with my son, and my girls were three and one, their dad left. I was afraid of going forward without God's help. My parents were far away after their retirement to Arizona, and they were dealing with Dad's health issues. I could no longer lean on them.

That's when I gave over the controls of my life to Christ. As I had learned so well in my growing-up years, it was the natural thing to do, the only solid place to turn. On a beautiful fall day in September 1985, I prayed, "God, I give You not just this situation— I give You my whole life. Do with it as You please."

That's when I began to see the miraculous evidenced in my own life. We moved from Indiana to Cincinnati, Ohio, in the fall of 1987, so that I could begin a doctoral program. My children were five, three, and one. There we started attending an Assembly of God church that helped us heal and get involved in worshiping as a family. And once again, the supernatural became normal; only this time that normal was mine instead of my parents'—really mine.

I would pray over my children at the beginning of each school year that God would keep flu away from our home. Season after season, as other kids dropped like flies, mine continued healthy and strong.

After the first year of my doctoral program, God spoke to me to buy a house. He went on to show me where, when and how much. It was truly amazing that Labor Day weekend when the realtor drove me to the house God had shown me. A few weeks later, it became our happy home.

I finished my doctorate in June 1990. Not knowing what to do next, I felt God tell me to apply for a position at the university

I'd just attended. I knew their rules for not hiring their own graduates until that person had been away at another institution for three years. Nevertheless, I took my résumé to the head of the education department, where he reminded me of their policies. But a short time later, he called. A position had opened up, and he invited me to become a visiting professor for that year. The job paid $25,000, enough for us to get by. But more importantly, because I was just a visiting professor, I would not be required to serve on committees, or counsel students. Therefore, my day was finished by 10:30 each morning.

My youngest child, Clint, was in kindergarten, and once again God spoke to me. He told me to start writing, and I did just that. I wrote whatever was in my hands: my testimony, called *Learning to Lean*; a book connecting my faith with my education, titled *Loving to Literacy*; and several children's books created from my son's speech therapy words. None of these works got published, but God would use them strategically in the days to come.

During the seven years we lived in Cincinnati, I began to realize that there were no limits on the ways God answered my prayers and showed Himself to me. Not once, but on three occasions I saw angels in our home. Each time they told me, "We've been sent to . . ." Once I awoke to a perfumed aroma in my bedroom. And I began to rely on the dreams and "leadings" God gave me to warn me or show me the next steps I should take. Those honeymoon times with God will always remain dear to my heart and foundational to my spiritual walk.

Big Changes

Then I felt things changing. I sensed that our connection with the home and church and the life we'd loved in Cincinnati was coming to an end. I had accepted a professor's position at the university in the town where I'd grown up, but something there had lost its allure as well.

One Monday night, on my birthday—February 14, 1994—I finished teaching a class and began my drive home. I cried out to God, acknowledging my awareness of His leading but also my confusion as to what He was calling me to do. I arrived home to a birthday cake the kids had made for me. After they went to bed, I knelt in front of the couch in our family room to continue my time with God. "Lord," I prayed, "if You truly are talking to me, speak louder!"

The next morning, I was widely awakened at 4:00. I turned on the light, pulled my Bible from the nightstand and asked God to speak to me from His Word. I opened to Isaiah 48:17: "I am the LORD your God, who teaches you to profit, who leads you by the way you should go." Then my eyes went to Isaiah 54:2-6, which read:

> Enlarge the place of your tent, and let them stretch out the curtains of your dwellings; do not spare; lengthen your cords, and strengthen your stakes. For you shall expand to the right and to the left, and your descendants will inherit the nations, and make the desolate cities inhabited. Do not fear, for you will not be ashamed; neither be disgraced, for you will not be put to shame; for you will forget the shame of your youth, and will not remember the reproach of your widowhood anymore. For your Maker is your husband, the LORD of hosts is His name; and your Redeemer is the Holy One of Israel; He is called the God of the whole earth. For the LORD has called you like a woman forsaken and grieved in spirit, like a youthful wife when You were refused.

As if these words had been written just for me, I knew that I had heard from God. I had received my instruction. The Holy Spirit had come through for me once again.

Three days later, I received a letter from Focus on the Family (where I knew no one) dated February 14, explaining that they'd seen some of my writing. What writing? The same writing the Holy Spirit directed me to start after He'd told me to take the part-time teaching position. The same writing that was turned down by a couple of publishers, but the same writing that made its way by one of the publishers to this vice president at Focus on the Family. The same writing that rang a bell with that man when he began his search for the editor of a new publication at Focus called *Single-Parent Family Magazine*.

The ministry flew me to Colorado Springs and offered me the position later that week. I finished some speaking jobs I had booked and my semester teaching at the university. Later, Focus on the Family flew me back to Colorado to find a home, and I started preparing for the sale of our house in Ohio. I guessed at a price, put an ad in the paper, received one reply and managed to delay the interested party until Easter Sunday, after I'd had time to organize our unfinished basement. A realtor was scheduled to come on Monday to list our home, but I preferred to sell it outright. So once again, we made it a matter of prayer. The kids and I prayed over air freshener and sprayed it throughout the house. Then we asked God for His favor.

That's exactly what happened. One ad. One man. One yes. One sale. And the price I guessed? It was the exact price of the appraisal. Then someone told me about an attorney who closed deals for home sales by owners. I called on him. When I explained that I was going to work for Focus on the Family, he offered his time and services at no cost.

On a Sunday at the end of May, my pastor had me deliver the morning sermon. That afternoon, a moving truck pulled into our driveway and packed our belongings. The following day, I headed out across country in our van with three kids and three animals. We smelled like Noah's Ark the next evening when we arrived in Colorado Springs to begin a new life.

If I Had It to Do Over . . .

I hit the ground running with my new job. Focus on the Family proved to be wonderful to me and provided radio, television, speaking and writing opportunities that I couldn't believe.

But I made a conscious choice then that I now regret. I decided to "sanitize" and "domesticate" my own walk with God. After all, I would be speaking and writing to people from all denominations of varying beliefs. Most hadn't seen the healings or heard God's voice or experienced the dreams and instructions the same way I had. I reasoned that the normal ways that God spoke and moved in my life were foreign to many. I convinced myself that people would close their ears to anything past "God showed me" or "God spoke to me" or "I had a dream."

I called it making the message "palatable." I tried to hold on to the deeper messages God *had* and *was* teaching me but deliver them in a more acceptable language. It's almost like I said to the Holy Spirit, "I believe in You in all kinds of ways, but many people that I'm now talking to don't. So climb in this drawer, and I'll let You know when to come out."

To some, my decision would be justified. But looking back, I now recognize that though it was the beginning of some good things in my life, it was the end of the miraculous. He stopped talking to me in the ways He'd done before. I no longer heard from God as I had previously. I lost that everyday, continuing dialogue with Him that I had found at cherished earlier times. Often I would speak to audiences without ever going to God to listen for His instruction. I also disregarded the special message I had to bring because of the unique relationship I'd found with Him. I realize now that when I demoted the Holy Spirit's role in my life, I also relinquished His power.

A New Day

Several years, books, articles, interviews and speeches later, I left Focus. I had remarried the year before, after more than 14 years as a single mom. The ministry had changed the direction of their magazines, so in July 2000, I finished out the last regular issue, said my good-byes, and turned my attention to writing full time.

The next five years saw five more published books, but I still had not regained the power I'd once known. In addition, after Dave and I married, we started attending a church that took me even further away from my roots. That church became representative of the very people I envisioned when I chose to stop sharing my own message. The longer we attended there, the more empty and lifeless I felt. Reading the Bible no longer gripped me, and I never, ever saw anyone healed or delivered as I had witnessed early on.

I did occasionally get a glimpse of what I had known. I became acquainted, for example, with a couple at the church where we attended who wanted children more than anything. After years of trying, they had all but given up. I asked to meet with them in a side room after church one Sunday morning. I showed them a bottle of anointing oil and described how some 35 years before, my grandfather had anointed and prayed for the pianist at our church who also faced infertility issues. She went on to have five children. I told this couple, "I don't know *how* it worked, but I know that it *did*."

And it worked again. A few weeks later, the woman called me to say she wanted me to be among the first to know that she was pregnant. Little Benjamin is now attending school.

So yes, God *was* with me. But I wanted more. I wanted to see His face and hear His voice and feel His presence again. I wanted more of the miraculous.

One morning, I was listening to praise music in my kitchen. I heard a song called, "You Are a God of Miracles." I bent over weeping and said, "God, I wouldn't know that if I hadn't seen it earlier with my own eyes. I want to see miracles and manifestations of Your power again!" I shared my heart at our home fellowship meeting later that week, but evidence of the miraculous continued to remain absent in my life.

Then one November day, I was returning from a hike with our dog. As I drove past one of the homes in our area, I noticed a family moving in. The husband stood on the driveway, so I stopped and introduced myself. He gave me his wife's email address; so in the weeks that followed, I invited them to attend our home fellowship, thinking I was doing some "evangelistic" work.

It was January before the wife came. Her name was Schlyce. Her husband had stayed home with their toddler because he had to get up early for work. Our normal group was there, and our normal routine took place; but what happened next was anything but normal. We went around the room with our same "tired" praying for one of the couples in the group. But when Schlyce started to pray, it was like someone handed me a glass of cold water. She prayed with confidence and anointing and power that I hadn't heard for a very long time. All I could do was cry.

As I got to know this woman and her ministry, I learned their story and the role of the Holy Spirit in their lives. She'd come to Jesus from what she called a "professional sinning" past. She'd eventually taken a position on staff with Bill Winston's 25,000-member congregation in Chicago. Then God spoke to them to move to Colorado Springs to start a prayer and healing ministry. God even showed them the exact house to move into—right next to me!

Now, I had learned that God speaks to His people. That was nothing new. I had even personally experienced that He shows exact houses for His people to move into. But to see that He chose that particular house right beside me for this couple to rent for a year and then move on told me that He still knew me. It told me that even more than I wanted to be with Him, He wanted to be with me. It told me that He had heard me and loved me and knew right where I was. It told me that He'd seen the cries and hunger of my heart for a living God. And most of all, it told me that at last the Holy Spirit had been let back out of the drawer in my life.

In the months since then, I have sat under intense teaching and studied extensively on my own, learning and relearning all I could about the Holy Spirit. This book is the result of that study and my newfound relationship. This book is also dedicated to You, Holy Spirit, the Gentleman that You are. You have waited patiently for me to allow You to become bigger in my life. And now You are.

When I chose to relegate the Holy Spirit's role in my world, I misplaced the very Thing that was the source of all other good things. Never again. I *will* make up for lost time. I *will* learn everything He has to teach me and share and demonstrate Him in any and every way He sees fit. I *will* spend the rest of my days whetting other people's appetite for the more. I *will* become His mouthpiece. And I *will* expect to see the miracles to come: "Therefore, behold,

I will again do a marvelous work among this people, a marvelous work and a wonder" (Isa. 29:14).

Welcome back, Holy Spirit.

ℳake It Yours
Understand Your Story

You've heard my story, now let's talk about yours. Imagine, if you will, the timeline of history. It begins with creation and ends with God's people living forever with Him. In between, fill in relevant events that have impacted history—including the birth, life, death and resurrection of Jesus. What else might you add?

Creation

_____

_____

_____

_____

_____

_____

Eternity

Now go back to the timeline above and fill in the presence of the Holy Spirit during each part of that history as you learned it in chapter 2 (e.g., the Holy Spirit's role at creation and throughout the Old and New Testaments). Think through the Holy Spirit's activity in *your* life. Somewhere on that timeline is a dot that belongs to you. The assignment for your time and your place on earth is just as specific and ordained and planned out as it was for Moses or Joshua or Esther or Ruth. Mark your "spot" on the timeline and envision it always from this point on.

Now reflect back on evidence (or lack of evidence) of the Holy Spirit's work in you during the various decades of your life and write this in the space below. Think hard. Also note those times you may not have recognized His work then, but you see it now.

Ages 0–10

_____
_____
_____

Ages 11–20

_____
_____
_____

Ages 21–30

_____
_____
_____

Ages 31–40

_____
_____
_____

Other

_____
_____
_____

Write a summary paragraph about the movement of the Holy Spirit since your birth.

_____
_____
_____

This week, memorize the following verses to remind you of the Holy Spirit's activity in your life and of how special and unique you are to God:

> I will praise You, for I am fearfully and wonderfully made; marvelous are Your works, and that my soul knows very well (Ps. 139:14).

> The steps of a good man are ordered by the LORD, and He delights in his way. Though he fall, he shall not be utterly cast down; for the LORD upholds him with His hand. I have been young and now am old; yet I have not seen the righteous forsaken, nor his descendants begging bread (Ps. 37:23-25).

> Blessed be the God and Father of our Lord Jesus Christ, who has blessed us with every spiritual blessing in the heavenly places in Christ, just as He chose us in Him before the foundation of the world, that we should be holy and without blame before Him in love, having predestined us to adoption as sons by Jesus Christ to Himself, according to the good pleasure of His will, to the praise of the glory of His grace, by which He made us accepted in the Beloved (Eph. 1:3-6).

I can't let this last verse pass without sharing with you a beautiful bit of information. "Accepted in the Beloved" is actually the same word the angel uses in Luke 1:28 when he is speaking about Mary, the mother of Jesus: "Rejoice, highly favored one, the Lord is with you; blessed are you among women!" The angel goes on to describe the Holy Spirit's work in this humanly impossible situation when he tells Mary, "The Holy Spirit will come upon you, and the power of the Highest will overshadow you; therefore, also, that Holy One who is to be born will be called the Son of God" (Luke 1:35).

The same word translated as "highly favored" (Luke 1:28) and "accepted in the Beloved" (Eph. 1:6) appear only these two times in Scripture. From this, the conclusion can be drawn that there are only two people in God's sight who are highly favored and accepted in the Beloved: Mary and you. Hallelujah!

PRAYER CONFESSION

Holy Spirit, thank You that I am fearfully and wonderfully made. Thank You that You chose me before the foundation of the world to be adopted as a daughter by Jesus Christ to Himself. Thank You that, like Mary, I am accepted in the Beloved, highly favored. Thank You that I now see my life as a narrative in which You are very much involved. Thank You that You have been active and working in me since before I was born. Thank You that You have been aware of and engaged in everything that has happened to me. Thank You that You have brought me to this place of learning more about You and of finding a more secure and personal relationship with You in every aspect of my life. And thank You that You are leading me in my steps forward and that the days ahead of me are not left to chance. Thank You that I am more in tune with Your voice and that I won't miss any instruction You have for me. In Jesus' name. Amen.

4

*T*wice the Impact

He said to them, "Did you receive the Holy Spirit when you believed?" So they said to him, "We have not so much as heard whether there is a Holy Spirit."
ACTS 19:2

I did some speaking once with a man who described a method he used for maintaining his right priorities. The top of his roll-top desk showcased pictures of the most important events and people in his life. His efforts began on the left with snapshots of the hospital where he was born and ended on the right with the burial plot where his body would one day rest. In between, photos of his wife, children and grandchildren were prominently displayed. These constant reminders helped him make right choices about the ways to divide his time and efforts among these most essential things as he continued to live his life. If an issue, project or individual didn't belong among those high-ranking items presented, it didn't deserve his attention and resources, and he returned his focus to the things that did.

Corny as this exercise may seem, it has kept me thinking, through the years, about the personalized display that belongs to each of us. Though not atop a roll-top desk, God has created His own pictorial representation of your life.

Before you were ever born, God mapped out your life. He began with a picture of the exact plans He assigned to you before the foundation of the world (see Eph. 1:4). He ended with the scene of you spending eternity with Him after your assigned work has been accomplished. In between these times are the date, time and location of your most important decision—accepting Jesus as your Savior and Lord and welcoming the Holy Spirit to live inside you. And because your heavenly Father adores giving things to His kids, He also added many similar pictures such as those my friend included—graduations, wedding days and children's births—mementoes of beautiful gifts that have graced your world.

But there is yet another gift, one that perhaps you were not aware of and may not have opened: "If you then, being evil, know how to give good gifts to your children, how much more will your heavenly Father give the Holy Spirit to those who ask Him!" (Luke 11:13).

God extends the gift of the Holy Spirit in an added dimension to His children who dare to seek Him for this coveted prize, and then the picture of the moment when you were baptized in the Holy Spirit joins the others in your personalized display. This gift has nothing to do with your eternal destination as it did when you were born again and received the Holy Spirit. Instead, this additional measure of the Holy Spirit provides for your abundant life here and now (see John 10:10). Receipt of this gift enables you to become an active participant rather than just a passive observer in everything else that will happen to you for the rest of your life. It puts power in your praying. Through the Holy Spirit, you can gain God's mind and wisdom for a thriving, victorious life instead of just a surviving one.

Many Christians don't know they can have the Holy Spirit in this capacity. They stop with the salvation experience. They're taught that all they are ever going to get from the Holy Spirit happens at the time they are born again. But there is more, so very much more, and Jesus prayed for the "more" in this verse:

And I will pray the Father, and He will give you another Helper, that He may abide with you forever—the Spirit of truth, whom the world cannot receive, because it neither sees Him nor knows Him; but you know Him, for He dwells *with* you and will be *in* you (John 14:16-17, emphasis added).

Your relationship with God only begins at salvation when the Holy Spirit comes to be *with* you at salvation; but it continues when He comes to live *in* you as you grow. Let's see just how that comes about.

Impact 1: With You—Born *of* the Spirit

You read in chapter 2 how the Holy Spirit left after sin entered the world and, as recorded throughout the Old Testament, returned only for brief visits. He came "upon" specific people to accomplish specific otherwise-impossible tasks for a specific period of time. The Holy Spirit no longer came to stay until Jesus invaded the earth.

During Jesus' three-year ministry, He encountered a man named Nicodemus, who was a ruler of the Jews and a member of the Sanhedrin. As a Pharisee, Nicodemus was thoroughly trained in Jewish law and theology. He was drawn to the miraculous works Jesus had done, and he acknowledged them and attributed them to God being with Him. Jesus answered a question Nicodemus didn't even ask, and that answer remains to this day a basic tenet of our faith: "Unless one is born again, he cannot see the kingdom of God" (John 3:3).

You must be born again. Every Christian is familiar with this phrase "born again," but do you really know what it means? What happens when you are born again?

"Again" means "from above." The first time you are born (from your mother's womb), you are born physically. The second time you are born (or born again), you experience a spiritual birth from above. It's the Greek word *sozo,* and it means "material and temporal deliverance from danger and apprehension." It means "preservation, pardon, restoration, healing, wholeness and soundness." It's more than obtaining your ticket to heaven.

The Holy Spirit remains active during several stages of the salvation process:

- He's the One who "draws," pursues and compels you to come to Christ (see John 6:44).
- He makes your human spirit a new creation in Christ (see 2 Cor. 5:17).
- He bears witness with your spirit that you are a child of God (see Rom. 8:14,16).

You came into the world—born as a sinner, separated from God's Spirit—not because of *your* sin but because of your relationship with the first man, Adam. You had to go through a new birth to come alive in the work of the Holy Spirit. Through the new birth, you literally entered into a different realm where God's new Kingdom order could be realized (see 2 Cor. 5:17). It's more than being "saved." It again qualified you to the supernatural dimension of life and fit you for a beginning in God's Kingdom order. It's a huge deal! The process is laid out in Ephesians:

> In Him you also *trusted*, after you *heard* the word of truth, the gospel of your salvation; in whom also, having *believed*, you were *sealed* with the Holy Spirit of promise, who is the *guarantee* of our inheritance until the redemption of the purchased possession, to the praise of His glory (Eph. 1:13-14, emphasis added).

First, you *heard* the truth.
Second, you *trusted*.
Third, you *believed*.
Fourth, you were *sealed* with the Holy Spirit of promise.
You know that faith comes by hearing the Word of God (see Rom. 10:17). Sometime, somewhere, somehow, you heard the gospel. For Curt, it was on a plane flying into Colorado Springs, seated beside Dave, more than 10 years ago. Curt heard for the first time about salvation and being born again as Dave showed

him specific Bible verses. Curt became a new believer before the plane landed. Curt heard the truth and chose to believe. It was an option. The response was left to him.

Salvation may occur all at once, as it did for Curt after he heard the truth one time, or it may take multiple times after lots of people sow lots of seeds. For those who grow up in Christian homes, they hear and hear and hear the truth. Eventually, they have to believe for themselves, as there are no stepchildren in heaven. However varied the process, it takes place in the same order: First you hear, third you believe; but in between, you trust.

Something in you, which you now know to be the Holy Spirit, caused you to hope in or gravitate toward the gospel message. "Trusted" is the Greek word *proelpizo,* and it means "to hope in advance of other confirmation." Hunger draws you to eat. Exhaustion draws you to sleep. Trust draws you to believe. Trust was the warm-up that prepared you to accept the truth you heard. It's also called "first trust." It softened the hard ground of your heart to accept the seeds of salvation.

Then you believed. Really believed! You weren't slightly convinced of something. Instead, you became persuaded of. You placed your confidence in. You committed to. You developed faith *in* and *upon* with respect to that person or thing. Think about that. You weren't a believer, and then you were. And before that process could happen, certain things had to be put in place. The Truth had to be heard by the person (you) made ready through trust by the Holy Spirit. The day you believed didn't happen out of nowhere. It was a holy setup. That event for Curt had been in process long before he took his seat beside Dave on that plane. The Holy Spirit was busy at work lining up things so Curt could become a member in the family of God for eternity.

It could be said that the Holy Spirit had ulterior motives in doing what He did. He wanted to move into a new house within you—and that's exactly what happened at your believing salvation moment (see 1 Cor. 6:19). Not the makeshift tent of meeting that Moses erected for the Holy Spirit to dwell in, over which the cloud covered by day and the fire by night. This verse also doesn't refer to the elaborate temple Solomon built to house the Holy Spirit. We don't need either of those anymore. Instead, when we accept Jesus as Lord of our life, the Holy Spirit moves into flawed you and me, who sometimes overeat and lose our temper.

And His job doesn't stop there. Something else wonderful occurs. The Holy Spirit seals that new and wonderful thing that takes place at salvation. The word "seal" has a special meaning to me because of the gardens we grew when I was a child. On much of our acre of land in that small Ohio college town where we lived, we grew fruits and vegetables. My parents assigned us our chores in the upkeep of the produce. We planted, weeded and picked at all the appropriate times. Cucumbers turned into 14-day pickles, which stood in a crock on the counter. Corn was cut and scraped off the cob and scooped into freezer bags. There were also the processing of beets and peaches and berries, which found a place in our regular summer routines.

It was the green beans, however, that I think about when I hear the word "seal." We would pick 'em, wash 'em, string 'em and snap 'em on a magazine while we watched *Wagon Train* on TV. Next, Mom would stuff the beans into Ball jars, add water, place a rubber ring around the top of the jar, screw on the lid and place them carefully into the water in the pressure cooker. Once the cooking was complete and the jars were cooled, Mom would line them up in neat rows on our pantry shelf.

Some of my most vivid lessons learned throughout that process, however, took place during the winter. When Mom grabbed a jar of beans off the shelf and found the red rubber seal had been broken, she threw away the contents without further examination. Like breaking the seal on a liter of Coke or a bottle of ketchup, Mom knew that without the seal, spoilage ensued.

The Holy Spirit becomes that needed seal to preserve everything that happened inside you after you heard, trusted and then believed to salvation. It provides a forever shelf life. It allows the contents to stand the test of time instead of becoming a passing fad or a momentary emotion. "To seal" means to "to stamp with a signet or private mark for security, preservation and permanence." This seal is like a wedding ring of sorts, which tells everyone that you are taken—"spoken for" for the rest of your life. It lays claim to you. It confirms your permanent ownership into the heavenly family. The Holy Spirit's investment in you is God's title to possessing you entirely and forever!

But that's still not all. The Holy Spirit serves one more role at the time of the born-again experience:

> [He] is the guarantee of our inheritance until the redemption of the purchased possession, to the praise of His glory (Eph. 1:14).

The Holy Spirit becomes a "guarantee"—a deposit, downpayment, first installment, earnest money—until you can receive the full amount of your reward some day! There's more to come. It's kind of like the girl handing out food samples at the mall food court, whose intent is to let you know about the delicious stuff waiting for you just across the counter. She wants to make you hungry for more. The seal-guarantee-upon experience is a tangible, visible harbinger of what lies ahead, to let you know you ain't seen nothin' yet, and to keep you anchored and focused on the eternal.

I don't know about you, but I almost have to stop for a moment to grasp how busy the Holy Spirit has been behind the scenes in my life:

> Then Peter said to them, "Repent, and let every one of you be baptized in the name of Jesus Christ for the remission of sins; and you shall receive the gift of the Holy Spirit" (Acts 2:38).

But it's all part of the "with" experience of the Holy Spirit. The hearing-trusting-believing-sealing born-again experience process birthed you into the Spirit realm as a new creature in Christ. It is only step one of this miraculous provision, however.

Impact 2: In You—Baptized *in* the Spirit

So the Holy Spirit offers Himself as a guarantee of the unbelievably glorious things that are yet to come. But between getting to know Him through the born-again experience and someday living with Him, the Holy Spirit offers a deeper glimpse into the reality of who He can become. It's kind of like flying in an airplane. There are the regular coach passengers and the elite first-class passengers. Both are headed for the same place, but the method of travel is much different. One ticket holder takes what she can get in the back (if she's lucky, that might include a small bag of pretzels), while the person up front is aided and assisted for all her needs throughout the duration of the flight.

The same Spirit that came to dwell in you when you were born again shows up but in a deeper dimension to aid and assist you in life. He allows you to enter into the fullness of what God has for you, and it happens subsequent to being born again. That's why it's sometimes called "a separate experience."

The book of Acts calls the process "receiving," "being filled with" and "being baptized in" the Holy Spirit. Whether receiving, filling or baptizing with the Holy Spirit—every time the event occurred, it did so after the person had been born again. Let's take a look at two examples where this was true:

The Samaritans

The first instance is found in Acts 8:12-17:

> When they believed Philip as he preached the things concerning the kingdom of God and the name of Jesus Christ, both men and women were baptized. Then Simon himself also believed; and when he was baptized he continued with Philip, and was amazed, seeing the miracles and signs which were done. Now when the apostles who were at Jerusalem heard that Samaria had received the word of God, they sent Peter and John to them, who, when they had come down, prayed for them that they might receive the Holy Spirit. For as yet He had fallen upon none of

them. They had only been baptized in the name of the Lord Jesus. Then they laid hands on them, and they received the Holy Spirit.

Notice that Philip went to Samaria to preach Jesus; he didn't go there to preach the Holy Spirit. Why? Christ is to be preached to the world so they can be born again, but the Holy Spirit is to be preached and administered to believers (see Luke 11:13). Remember, the Holy Spirit is God's very special gift to His very special children who ask for it; but Jesus is God's gift to the world (see John 3:16). You must be born again before you can receive the infilling of the Holy Spirit (see John 14:16-17). All this would not be so if you received all of the Holy Spirit you were going to get at salvation.

So these Samaritans heard Jesus preached, then they trusted and believed, as evidenced in verse 12, when "both men and women were baptized" and in verse 14 "the apostles . . . heard that Samaria had received the word of God." And because Scripture later tells us that everyone who receives Jesus gets the right to become children of God (see John 1:12), we must conclude that these Samaritans were born again.

Next we read that Peter and John went to them and prayed that they would also "receive the Holy Spirit, for as yet He had fallen upon none of them. They had only been baptized in the name of the Lord Jesus" (vv. 15-16). Peter and John lay hands on them, and they received this subsequent, separate measure of the Holy Spirit.

Saul

Then there was Saul, whose name was later changed to Paul. He heard, trusted and believed while traveling on the road to Damascus. His is an example that makes you shake your head as you realize how the Holy Spirit was working on him all along. His heart was being softened toward the gospel and he was being prepared to trust and believe—even while he was still being hard on *other* people who believed! Makes you want to recommit to praying for the most hopeless sinner you know, doesn't it? Here is how it went down for Saul:

> Then Saul, still breathing threats and murder against the disciples of the Lord, went to the high priest and asked letters from him to the synagogues of Damascus, so that if he found any who were of the Way, whether men or women, he might bring them bound to Jerusalem. As he journeyed he came near Damascus, and suddenly a light shone around him from heaven. Then he fell to the ground, and heard a voice saying to him, "Saul, Saul, why are you persecuting Me?" And he said, "Who are You, Lord?" Then the Lord said, "I am Jesus, whom you are persecuting. It is hard for you to kick against the goads." So he, trembling and astonished, said, "Lord, what do You want me to do?" Then the Lord said to him, "Arise and go into the city, and you will be told what you must do." And the men who journeyed with him stood speechless, hearing a voice but seeing no one. Then Saul arose from the ground, and when his eyes were opened he saw no one. But they led him by the hand and brought him into Damascus. And he was three days without sight, and neither ate nor drank (Acts 9:1-9).

Paul later wrote to the Romans to tell them about the hearing/trusting/believing born-again process: "If you confess with your mouth the Lord Jesus and believe in your heart that God has raised Him from the dead, you will be saved" (Rom. 10:9). But for now, Saul knew only that something miraculous had happened to him, and he believed in it. He also obeyed. He went from giving orders to taking orders from Jesus. As he was told, he traveled to the city, prayed and waited for three days to hear what God would say to him. Meanwhile, the Holy Spirit was busy at work instructing a man named Ananias to also go to the city and lay hands on Saul:

> And Ananias went his way and entered the house; and laying his hands on him he said, "Brother Saul, the Lord

Jesus, who appeared to you on the road as you came, has sent me that you may receive your sight and be filled with the Holy Spirit" (Acts 9:17).

Saul had already believed and received Jesus, so Ananias called him "brother." Ananias was sent to Saul not for him to be born again, but so that his post-born-again, separate experience would include having his sight restored and filling him with the Holy Spirit.

Like the Samaritans and Saul, our Christian journey begins at the "with you," born-*of*-the-Spirit experience. It continues with the "in you," baptized-*in*-the-Spirit experience. But it still doesn't stop there. It continues as you take what you have received and share it with others.

Out of You—Empowered *by* the Spirit

Every Monday morning at my kitchen sink, I fill a plastic pitcher with water and then make the rounds to all my houseplants. When I return to the kitchen, I usually find something to do while the pitcher is refilling. But even when I'm busy eating or cooking, I watch to see when the pitcher gets full so it won't overflow onto my counter and floor. I know the rule that before you can put more in, you've got to let some out.

The same principle applied in the Old Testament when Moses was on Mount Horeb seeing God face to face and receiving the 10 Commandments. Who wouldn't want to keep being filled up by the things he saw? But God spoke to him and said, "You have dwelt long enough at this mountain" (Deut. 1:6). In other words, "It's time to go down and tell the others what I've shown you up here."

Peter, James and John learned a similar truth on Mount Hermon. "[Jesus] was transfigured before them. His face shone like the sun, and His clothes became as white as the light" (Matt. 17:2-3). In addition, two men (Moses and Elijah), who had died hundreds of years before, showed up to join them! Peter's response was much like yours and mine might have been. He wanted to remain in the moment by building three tabernacles as semi-permanent dwelling places. But we go on to read that down below was an epileptic boy needing to be healed, and multitudes waiting to be taught. What Peter, James and John got poured into them was no more meant to be kept to themselves than it was for Moses or even for my water pitcher. This fact is also true for you.

I call it "ministry in, ministry out." Both are necessary. You must fill the pitcher before you have something to pour out. On the other hand, you can't keep putting water in without allowing some to flow out. After you have received the "upon" experience through your new birth and the "in" experience through the baptism in the Holy Spirit, you are ready for the Holy Spirit to flow from *you* to *others*.

Pour the Same Out to Others

For the believers in the Early Church described in the book of Acts, little is said about their born-again "with" experience. That's probably because it's a deep, quiet, personal, eternal change that takes place inside the individual and is the foundation from which everything else grows. But just as soon as believers were filled with the Holy Spirit in the Upper Room (see Acts 2:2-4), a river began to flow out of them to others. First, ministry in; then ministry out. First, the Holy Spirit *with*; then the Holy Spirit *in*. Of the Holy Spirit, *in* the Holy Spirit, then *by* the Holy Spirit. That's when believers were added daily by the hundreds, and the gospel spread throughout the world.

What an amazing, intricate process God instituted when He gave us the Holy Spirit! The One who only showed up after the Fall for occasional visits set down roots after Jesus went away, and those roots grew deep in the hearts of everyone who made Jesus Lord of their lives. That same Holy Spirit wooed you, softened you, exposed you, helped you to believe, sealed you and then promised you the best was yet to come. Now He's continuing to take you deeper while allowing you to see more and more of who He is and who He wants to become in your life.

No wonder He now asks you to pour the same out to others. The news is too good to keep to yourself!

---

*M*ake It Yours
Welcome His Impact

Your life will never be all it was intended to be until you encounter all three dimensions of your life in Christ—*of, in* and *by* the Holy Spirit. Take some time and think through these dimensions as they pertain to you. Access where you *are* and where you *need to go* in each:

With You—Born-*of*-the-Spirit Experience

Many Christians never have a life-changing encounter with Jesus Christ. It's not enough to be religious, get baptized in water or take Communion. You read in this chapter how elaborate the process is and how much behind-the-scenes preparation it takes before someone actually comes to Christ. The well of water Jesus used to illustrate the new birth represents the continuous reservoir of God's Spirit within you and the restoration of the two-way communication from heaven to earth and earth to heaven.

Which phrase(s) most accurately describes the way you were taught to think about the born-again experience?

- ❑ Walk the aisle
- ❑ "Join" rather than "be birthed into"
- ❑ Get saved from damnation
- ❑ Receive your ticket to heaven
- ❑ Experience your spirit becoming one with God's Spirit
- ❑ Gain citizenship to a new Kingdom with new power and benefits
- ❑ Other:

Review the "Born of the Spirit" section of this chapter. What actually happened in the spirit realm when you prayed the sinner's prayer?

_____

_____

_____

_____

Write out Luke 15:10, which paints a picture of the party that is thrown every time a person becomes a new believer.

_____

_____

_____

_____

Which statement best describes your born-again experience?

- ❑ You've never had one.
- ❑ You feel more like you eloped with Jesus instead of taking part in the huge wedding celebration that you were entitled to.
- ❑ That moment is forever etched in your heart and mind, and you would do nothing different.
- ❑ You would like to take part in a ceremony to renew your vows and, in the process, experience and solidify everything you missed the first time.

In You—Baptized-*in*-the-Spirit Experience

Some Christians have a powerful born-again encounter with Jesus, but they spend the rest of their lives trying to live out of the flesh because they don't have the power of the Spirit at work inside of them. They haven't recognized the Holy Spirit's ability in this way; therefore, they can't cooperate with it. The baptism in the Holy Spirit restores your ability to carry out the authority God ordained you to have. It also gives you the power to prove the claims of the Bible and to bring them alive in your life and in the lives of those around you.

Do you believe in the baptized-*in*-the-Spirit experience? Have you learned something new about it? Explain.

Do you feel you have been baptized in/filled with the Holy Spirit? Why or why not?

As you have seen, getting "filled with the Spirit" is not a one-time process: "And do not be drunk with wine, in which is dissipation; but be filled with the Spirit" (Eph. 5:18). The verb tense used in this passage for "be filled" indicates that being filled with the Spirit does not involve a single experience. It is maintained by continuing to fill it. If you have already experienced the baptism in/filling with the Holy Spirit, how have you kept that filling full?

Have you been successful in this area? Why or why not? How might you make your continuing infilling more effective?

If you have never been baptized in or filled with the Holy Spirit, ask God to fill you right now.

Out of You—Empowered-by-the-Spirit Experience
Ministry in through the *in* and *with* work of the Holy Spirit prepares
you for your ministry *out*. How has the Holy Spirit's impact in your
life affected your impact on others?

_____

_____

_____

_____

After reading this chapter, what are three ways you can share this
good news about the Holy Spirit? With whom can you share it?

_____

_____

_____

_____

PRAYER CONFESSION

*Holy Spirit, thank You that as You did with Saul, You wooed me
and made me ready to receive Christ; then You came to live inside me when I believed for myself. Thank You that You have led
me to this place where I'm now learning even more about You.
Thank You that You're teaching me to include You in every aspect of my life. And thank You that You are leading me to share
what I have learned with others—what to share, how to share it
and who to share it with. Thank You that You have come alive in
me. Thank You that I will never, ever be the same again—and
it's all because of You. In Jesus' name, amen.*

5

$\mathscr{T}$he Big T

Therefore, brethren, desire earnestly to prophesy,
and do not forbid to speak with tongues.
1 CORINTHIANS 14:39

I went for a long-overdue appointment the other day to get my eyebrows waxed (you know the urgency in that task). As Soncha worked on me, I asked questions about her life. I knew she was a Christian, so I inquired how she'd come to know Jesus, and she told me her story.

Soncha was born in Korea as one of seven children and lost her parents when she was 18. Her whole family was Buddhist, and Shamanism (where they communicated with the spiritual world) and witchcraft (which was used to cast spells on them because of the Catholic school she and her siblings attended) were among the many pagan beliefs common in their home. Soncha wanted to break free. She blamed Buddhism for damaging her family and country. She decided that marrying a GI was her only escape, so she asked a soldier named Leon (whom she'd been dating for a short time) to marry her. The question scared him away for a month, but they married nine months later, in 1976. She decided that when they arrived in America, she would find the real God since the ones she'd known to this point had failed her.

Once they moved to Texas, the Holy Spirit stepped up His work in her life. A friend invited her to church, and Soncha found

Christian TV. She began her own search and decided to try a Korean Nazarene church someone had recommended. She cried uncontrollably as soon as she walked through the door. She went home and told God, "I don't want anything from You. I just want to know You. If You don't work, nothing will." She continued to attend the church, and the more she learned, the more she realized she didn't know. That included how to pray.

So she began a routine of getting alone with God at 9:00 P.M. in her clothes closet. She talked with Him about everything she could think of—past, present and future. "Suddenly," she said, "my tongue started slipping, moving, speaking in a language I didn't know. I couldn't stop, and I knew I wasn't smart enough to do it on my own. I even bit my tongue a couple of times to make it stop. But it kept happening every time I went into my closet to pray."

At the same time, the Bible started opening up to Soncha a little at a time, and she began to notice things inside her that needed to change. Eventually she went to her pastor and told him what was happening to her when she prayed, but he shot her down with responses such as "not real" and "Satan uses tongues to manipulate our minds."

But it was real to Soncha, very real, and it continued to happen. She talked to God there and listened as He talked with her. That experience began her nearly three-decade dynamic journey of faith, and speaking in tongues became an integral part of it all.

Mum's the Word for Tongues

The response Soncha received from her pastor is indicative of the Body of Christ as a whole. Tongues is the most divisive aspect of the Holy Spirit. Christians—and indeed, whole denominations—discount tongues and its relationship to the Holy Spirit. And because the Holy Spirit is a Gentleman and will not force His activity on anyone, we see tongues largely absent in our churches today.

The topic of tongues *is* important and must be addressed. I will devote this chapter only to the issue of tongues and will not pose a theological debate. I will simply discuss the topic and examine the Scriptures as I have come to understand them—both personally and through people like Soncha that I have known. I prefer approaching it that way, the simple way ("the simplicity that is in Christ" [2 Cor. 11:3]). Nothing could be simpler and less controversial than the closet experience Soncha had. Speaking in tongues purely and simply happened to Soncha as an outgrowth of her seeking and loving her Savior.

In essence, that's where I come down on the issue. Since my childhood, I have experienced the natural inclusion of tongues as a part of what the Holy Spirit offers God's people as a means to the end of heaven-to-earth communication. I have also both worked and worshiped extensively on the side of the aisle with wonderful Christians who oppose tongues. Thing is, so many people who resist speaking in tongues also admit they don't really know much about it. My job in this chapter is to present the evidence. Your job is to carefully look at all of that evidence and then prayerfully decide where the Holy Spirit might be leading you in this area. The beauty in both is that God knows our hearts and our desires to earnestly seek out everything He has to give us. And that begins with a concentrated look at what speaking in tongues really means and what it might have to offer you.

Our Common History of Common Language

According to a national report by the U.S. English Foundation, there are 322 different languages spoken in the United States. Despite the diversity, however, we are united under one common language—English. A common language is necessary for a nation to evolve and grow. A common language promotes communication and understanding within organizations. Imagine that you were in a serious automobile accident, and five first responders arrived on the scene. What if those five workers didn't share a common language? Words such as "neck brace" or "stretcher" or "synthetic blood platelets" to stop your bleeding would mean five different things to these five people. You'd find yourself in a heap of trouble.

Common language. It's important for everything from information sharing to nation building. It's the key to a person's national identity. It gives people a shared perspective not only on life, but also on how that life is expressed. It signifies a common heritage and a generational transfer.

It is also important to the victorious Christian life. Tongues is considered the common language between heaven and earth, between God and His people. When the Holy Spirit indwells our lives, we are offered the privilege of *hearing* His presence. It is manifest in the evidence of language; and tongues isn't just reserved for emergencies such as the one mentioned above. Yes, tongues is an essential tool desperately needed in a crisis; but mostly, tongues is the means by which regular communication takes place and relationship grows on an individual basis. In the process, the strangeness of tongues disappears as its true and vital purpose becomes clear.

In the beginning, conversations between God and the first man and woman flowed effortlessly: "The LORD God commanded the man, saying . . ." (Gen. 2:16); "and the LORD God said . . ." (Gen. 2:18). But another huge cost of the Fall was man's ongoing language and relationship with God. The situation reminds me of my best post-college friend. We lived in the same apartment complex, talked every day and discussed common stages in our lives. Then I moved away and was really bad about staying in touch. We didn't talk. We lost our intimacy. Now our relationship ceases to exist.

Not long after Adam, the common language between heaven and earth ceased as well. The post-Fall man had attempted to live life apart from God, but the earth had continued to speak one language. By the time of Genesis 11:1-9, however, we read about a man named Nimrod, who set himself up as the first ruler-dictator in history. He oversaw the building of a city and a tower in his kingdom of Shinar (also known as Babylon), "whose top is in the heavens" (v. 4). The purpose was to make a name for the Babylonians and prevent them from scattering throughout the earth.

But the Lord came down and observed the city and tower they had built. Even God recognized and acknowledged the unlimited strength and power that came from speaking a common language. He said, "'Indeed the people are one and they all have one language . . . *now nothing that they propose to do will be withheld from them*. Come, let Us go down and there confuse their language, that they may not understand one another's speech" (Gen. 11:6-7, emphasis added).

Speaking a common language made them too strong, even without God. So He put a stop to it and scattered them across the face of the earth. They named the tower "Babel," which means "mixed or confused," because there the Lord confused the language of all the earth. But that confusion would not always remain. Fast-forward to a prophecy found later in the Old Testament:

> For then I will restore to the peoples a pure language, that they all may call on the name of the LORD, to serve Him with one accord (Zeph. 3:9).

Then there was the prophecy of the Holy Spirit being poured out:

> And it shall come to pass afterward that I will pour out My Spirit on all flesh; your sons and your daughters shall prophesy, your old men shall dream dreams, your young men shall see visions (Joel 2:28).

And then there was Pentecost and the actual arrival of the Holy Spirit, which brought these prophecies together:

> When the Day of Pentecost had fully come, they were all with one accord in one place. And suddenly there came a sound from heaven, as of a rushing mighty wind, and it filled the whole house where they were sitting. Then there appeared to them divided tongues, as of fire, and one sat upon each of them. And they were all filled with the Holy Spirit and began to speak with other tongues, as the Spirit gave them utterance (Acts 2:1-4).

Finally, we can't forget the end of the story and John's prophecy of the multitudes from all over the earth who would survive the great Tribulation and praise Jesus together in a common language once again (see Rev. 7:9-12).

After Babel, we had the prophecies of Zephaniah and Joel and what happened at Pentecost; *before* the fulfillment of the end times, believers have and will continue to encounter a unique experience that includes speaking in tongues. This ability to participate in a heaven-given language is one of the first things the Holy Spirit imparts after He infills us. It allows ordinary men and women to once more share a common tongue (see Acts 1:8; Mark 16:17-18; Acts 2:1-11). We find evidence of it first in the book of Acts.

Four "Acts" of Baptism

One of the arguments against speaking in tongues is that not everyone who is baptized in the Holy Spirit speaks in tongues. Following the outpouring of the Holy Spirit that we just examined in Acts 2:1-4, and the tongues that fell as a result, the book of Acts contains four more instances of people being baptized in the Holy Spirit. Let's take a look at these examples and the place that tongues did or did not play in each instance:

Philip and the Samaritans (Acts 8:4-25)

Philip preached Christ to the Samaritans, and they received the Holy Spirit (see 8:4-17). These verses don't tell us specifically that these people spoke in tongues, but we can infer that they did when we read in verse 18 that Simon the sorcerer "saw that through the laying on of the apostles' hands the Holy Spirit was given." Since the Holy Spirit can't be seen with our physical eyes, some other outward manifestation had to serve as proof. If tongues didn't accompany the baptism in the Holy Spirit, how did this unbeliever know the Samaritans had received it? Simon saw something and went on to offer money to Peter and John to "buy" the same thing he saw. He wanted to be able to minister the Holy Spirit to others. He wanted to "see" others be baptized in the Holy Spirit.

Saul of Tarsus: Acts 9:4-18

The story of Saul's born-again experience is found in Acts 9:4-9 and is evidenced by Saul immediately calling Jesus "Lord": "Lord, what do you want me to do?" (v. 6). Then we read about his separate experience of being filled with the Holy Spirit. As in the example before, this passage also does not say that Saul spoke in tongues, but we read later that he did: "I thank my God I speak with tongues more than you all" (1 Cor. 14:18). As a result, we can assume that Saul spoke in tongues after he was baptized in the Holy Spirit.

Cornelius and His Household: Acts 10:1-46

The impact continued 10 years after Pentecost as the gospel spread from only the Jews to include the Gentiles as well. A Roman military officer named Cornelius was praying one day when an angel appeared and told him to send someone to Joppa to find Peter at the home of Simon the tanner. When Peter arrived at Cornelius' home, he preached the gospel to them, and the Holy Spirit came on those who heard. Observing Jewish believers were astonished at how the gift of the Holy Spirit had been poured out on this Roman household. Once again, how did they know, since the Holy Spirit can't be physically seen? "For they heard them speak with tongues and magnify God" (Acts 10:46).

The Disciples at Ephesus: Acts 19:1-6

Another decade went by. The setting was Ephesus in Asia Minor, and the characters were the believers who were walking in the light and revelation they had up to that point. The media of the day was behind the times, so they hadn't yet heard about what had been happening in Israel and what the Holy Spirit had been doing since Pentecost. Paul preached to them and they were baptized. Then what happened? "And when Paul had laid hands on them, the Holy Spirit came upon them, and they spoke with tongues and prophesied" (Acts 19:6).

Tongues were specifically mentioned as evidence after being baptized in the Holy Spirit in two of the four examples over a 20-year

period, between the Day of Pentecost (see Acts 2) and Paul's encounter with the Ephesian believers (see Acts 19). In the other two
examples, the Bible infers that they spoke in tongues as well. The
correlation is clear. It's not enough, however, to see only what the
Holy Spirit *did;* we also need to understand what He *will do* and
what that means to your life today.

Eight Truths About the Gift of Tongues

The Bible tells us that we are strangers and pilgrims on earth (see
Heb. 11:13). We're just passing through. That means our real citizenship is from another place (heaven). It's where we've come
from, what we exist for and where we're headed. A friend of mine
is Chaldean (from southern Iraq). Even though she has lived in
America her whole life, she holds on to her roots and her language.
When she gets on the phone with family members in her homeland and starts speaking her native language, you'd never know
that she belongs to America.

Similarly, when you speak in tongues, it's as if you had picked
up the phone and called your Father in your home country and
spoken to Him in your native tongue. "For he who speaks in a
tongue does not speak to men but to God, for no one under-
stands him; however, in the spirit he speaks mysteries" (1 Cor.
14:2). Tongues is your direct line to heaven, where you speak *out*
of your spirit *through* your native tongue (regardless of where
you're living or what's happening to you), instead of speaking
with your mind.

Have you ever prayed in English and finished feeling dissatis-
fied? Have you ever felt as if you failed to get your need across and
haven't received the answer you sought? When the Holy Spirit
came to live inside you at the new birth, He began to guide you in
your prayers as much as He could. After you are filled with the
Holy Spirit and are able to speak in tongues, however, your prayer
life gets ramped up as the Holy Spirit's guidance becomes available in a far greater measure. But before taking the tongues lunge,
you need to understand at least eight truths about it.

Truth 1: The Gift of Tongues Wasn't Restricted to Just the Early Church

Many people who reject the baptism of the Holy Spirit insist it went away with the Early Church. They use 1 Corinthians 13:10 to support their claims: "But when that which is perfect has come, then that which is in part will be done away." They maintain that God only gave the gifts of the Holy Spirit to the Early Church because the Bible hadn't been completed as yet. But in context, Paul's reason for writing 1 Corinthians 12, 13 and 14 was to instruct them on correctly operating in the gifts of the Holy Spirit. "When that which is perfect is come" is referring to Jesus' second coming, not to the Bible. So until He comes here or you go there, tongues hasn't passed away. *But when that time arrives,* you won't need tongues because you'll see Him face to face and know Him completely. As long as your knowledge of Jesus is incomplete, you'll need the gifts of the Spirit, and that includes tongues (see 1 Cor. 14:39).

Truth 2: There Are Two Kinds of Tongues

Tongues come in two varieties: private and public. The purpose for both is edification (or building up). One is for the individual herself, and the other is for the corporate Body. One is for ministry *in*, the other for ministry *out* (see 1 Cor. 14:26). Public tongues is one of the gifts listed in 1 Corinthians 12 and 14, which we will discuss in more detail in chapter 9. The public gift of tongues in church requires interpretation (see 1 Cor. 14:27-28). But you can also pray to receive the ability to interpret your private tongues (see 1 Cor. 14:13).

Truth 3: Private Tongues Is Available to Every Spirit-filled Believer

Some people interpret 1 Corinthians 12:29-30 to mean that not everyone should speak in tongues. "Are all apostles? Are all prophets? . . . Do all speak with tongues? Do all interpret?" Paul isn't talking about the spiritual gifts that he wrote about in 1 Corinthians 12:1-11. Here he's talking about fivefold ministry gifts, which are only bestowed on a few. So no, not everyone possesses these public ministry gifts.

But Mark 16:17-18 tells us that the options greatly expand when it comes to the personal area: "These signs will follow those who believe: In My name they will cast out demons; they will speak with new tongues; . . . they will lay hands on the sick, and they will recover." If you're a Spirit-filled believer, you're a candidate not only to speak in tongues but also to be part of other miraculous works as well (see Acts 2:39).

Truth 4: Tongues Doesn't Force Its Way into Your Life

Tongues is not the baptism in the Holy Spirit, and the baptism in the Holy Spirit is not tongues. The Holy Spirit doesn't *make* you do anything. Speaking in tongues is a choice; not doing it doesn't mean that you haven't been baptized in the Holy Spirit. It *does* mean that you're missing out on something wonderful that is part of the infilling package and is yours for the taking—a direct two-way communication with heaven. Speaking in tongues provides immediate, audible proof of the Holy Spirit's filling in a believer, but it must be sought after (even if it is done so unknowingly as Soncha did through seeking intimacy with Jesus) before it can be received. So if you don't *want* tongues, you probably won't *get* tongues.

Truth 5: Fear Can Prevent You from Receiving

Faulty teaching resulting in fear and wrong attitudes toward tongues will similarly prevent you from receiving the Holy Spirit in full measure. Fear can also convince you that if you profess to be filled with the Holy Spirit and speak in tongues, you'll be branded as "weird" and be expected to perform the miraculous (see Mark 16:17-18). That's why we settle in to a comfortable, non-controversial place where we profess salvation and are on our way to heaven but don't exercise the supernatural-working power of the Holy Spirit apparent in others.

Believe me, I know that acceptable place. For years, I was a card-carrying member of the club for Christians who didn't make waves. I could only imagine being at church or in a social gathering and talking about His power and the specific work of the Holy

Spirit in my life. I persuaded myself that conversations (as well as relationships) would end at that revelation. What I didn't realize then is that as I mustered the courage to begin speaking more boldly (which also comes from the Holy Spirit, see Acts 4:31), others started speaking up as well. We began to share in diverse venues about the separate work of the Holy Spirit in our lives, and tongues became a part of that conversation.

Truth 6: The Holy Spirit Doesn't Speak in Tongues *Through* You
Tongues won't just start speaking on their own. The Holy Spirit doesn't blurt out tongues through you or *do* the praying on His own. Instead, He helps your spirit to pray. He's waiting for your will to kick into gear, then He *gives you* the utterance and you do the praying (see 1 Cor. 14:14, *AMP*). God has provided a way through tongues for us to pray apart from our understanding. In Acts 2:4, the Holy Spirit gave them utterance, but they did the talking. Paul wrote of speaking in tongues more than you all—*not* the Holy Spirit speaking through him more than you all (see 1 Cor. 14:18).

In the same way, we shouldn't wait for the Holy Spirit to speak in tongues *for* us but should yield to the urge to speak in tongues ourselves through the Spirit *in* us and then listen as He accomplishes His work. And by the way, don't worry about saying the wrong thing. Don't try to analyze what's coming out of your mouth. Release your tongue to the Holy Spirit; then in faith, say the words He's inspiring you to say. Speak the utterance He gives you. Open your mouth and speak out.

Truth 7: It's Not a One-time Thing
You don't just speak in tongues once as evidence that you've received the baptism in the Holy Spirit and then never do it again. Every time you speak in tongues following that initial experience, you will find refreshment, build yourself up in your most holy faith (see Jude 1:20) and keep the love of God alive in your heart—all over again. As you speak God's wisdom and mysteries and ask for the interpretation, revelation will start to come and tell you things that you couldn't get any other way. That's why Satan has

so strongly fought this gift. If you have it, you have understanding on a regular basis.

It requires, however, regularly speaking in tongues (see 1 Cor. 14:14). The Holy Spirit gives your spirit the ability to do so. He directs your prayer as He gives you utterance. He prays through you about things before those things ever happen (see John 16:13). Whatever He hears, He speaks to you through the Word and on the inside of you as you pray in tongues.

Truth 8: The Advantages Are Many
What will you receive as a result of being baptized in the Holy Spirit and speaking in tongues?

- *You will grow spiritually* (see 1 Cor. 14:2,4). Your faith grows when you receive answers after speaking your prayers to Him in tongues and seeing your prayers answered.

- *You will surround yourself in God's love* (see Jude 1:20-21). Speaking in tongues assists you with constantly being immersed in God's forever love for you.

- *You will receive rest and refreshment* (see Isa. 28:11-12). The part of you where God lives (your spirit) is righteous, holy, rested and refreshed; and when you pray in tongues, you pass on that refreshment to the rest of you (your soul and body).

- *You will find encouragement* (see Col. 3:16). As you press into God in tongues, encouragement will come as you realize God is still in charge of all things and is helping you become part of His provision.

- *You will communicate directly with God* (see 1 Cor. 14:14). Your Spirit *is* the very mind of Christ (see 1 Cor. 2:16; Col. 3:10; 1 John 2:20) and always prays correctly. It means the difference between praying from your intellect (with *incomplete* details of the Word of God and the situations involved) and praying from your spirit (with *complete* knowledge of all things).

• *You will intercede* (see Rom. 8:26-27). You don't know how to talk to God about the issue, so you pray in tongues, which enables you to step out of the flesh and into the spirit and pray exactly what you need.

• *You will speak God's wisdom* (see 1 Cor. 2:6-7; 14:2). The same wisdom that created all things becomes yours through speaking in tongues the very wisdom of God!

Speaking in tongues will also allow you to develop Kingdom identity, assist you in keeping your flesh under control instead of reacting to only what you can see with your physical eyes, and help you become thankful and worshipful. Doesn't that sound like something you would like to make part of your Christian walk? As Paul states, "I will also pray with the understanding. I will sing with the Spirit" (1 Cor. 14:15).

The Difference that Being Filled with the Spirit Makes

I don't pretend to know everything there is to know about the gift Jesus left us in the Holy Spirit and the wonderful gift *He* gives us through tongues. But I'm convinced that tongues *does* play and *will* play a major part in our direct communication with heaven as long as we are on this earth. Knowing the Holy Spirit through born-again experience is wonderful, but knowing the Holy Spirit through the baptism of the Holy Spirit is incredible! At the new birth, God introduced His life and nature to you. At the baptism in the Holy Spirit, He introduces His supernatural power, and tongues is an important part of that provision.

I would like to end this chapter with Angela's story about the difference that being filled with the Spirit and speaking in tongues made in her life:

Prior to being filled with the Holy Spirit and speaking in tongues, my walk and relationship with God was like communicating with someone underwater. It was cloudy, foggy and garbled. But once I invited the Holy Spirit into my life and allowed Him to work in me, *wow* was everything different! It was like color danced off the pages of the Bible. I easily understood the Word. It became vibrant and clear, and I could hear the voice of the Lord through the Holy Spirit speaking to me. What do ya know; I was getting personal revelation! I felt like I was going to burst. I was getting filled with the Word in a new way, and it was because of the Holy Spirit.

It was because of the Holy Spirit. That just about says it all!

---

*M*ake It Yours
Talk His Language

Some people believe that receiving the baptism in the Holy Spirit is difficult. Karen wrote, "I've been attending a charismatic church for 20 years, and still haven't spoken in tongues." If we are taught that receiving the baptism in the Holy Spirit is a valid, separate experience, we're often told we have to wait on and work for it. We're taught that we have to "travail."

In the space below, write out Acts 1:4-5.

_____

_____

_____

_____

Many people use the words in these verses to prove that God will fill us with the Holy Spirit only when He is good and ready and that we have nothing to do with the timing. They are also convinced that we have to be clean enough to receive the Holy Spirit in this way. But let's think about this for a minute. When Jesus told His disciples to wait for the baptism, the Holy Spirit had not yet been poured out upon the earth. Then came Pentecost.

Write out Acts 2:1,4. What happened at Pentecost?

_____

_____

_____

_____

Since you live in post-Pentecost times and the Holy Spirit has already been poured out, do you believe you have to wait, beg and tarry for Him to fill you? Why or why not?

_____

_____

_____

_____

Now write out Luke 11:13.

_____

_____

_____

_____

In this passage, you are reminded that the Holy Spirit is a gift. Because of that, it's free and you don't have to earn it. And what about feeling unworthy and not pure enough to be filled with the Holy Spirit? The truth is that if you could rid yourself of all sin, you wouldn't need the Holy Spirit. Write out Luke 11:10-12:

_____

_____

_____

_____

_____

Based on these verses, what conclusions can you draw about being baptized in the Holy Spirit?

_____

_____

_____

_____

Now just might be the time to go that step further in your walk with God to be baptized in the Holy Spirit and speak in tongues. Regardless of your prior teaching and experience, you can do that today. Based on what you've learned about tongues, what might you have to lose? What might you have to gain?

_____

_____

_____

_____

Here's how one reader described what she did when she came to the point you are now:

> It all began with a hunger for more of something. I felt something was missing, and I was dissatisfied with where religion had taken me. Then I began to read some out-of-the-box books about this Thing or Person called the Holy Spirit that would have been considered blasphemous in my circle of Christian friends. Some of what I read seemed over the top but yet it was so real, so easy, so inviting. One author said, "Don't take what I am saying and just believe me, but seek God for your own personal revelation." I did exactly that. As I talked to God about all I was learning, it became obvious that He wanted me to be filled with the Holy Spirit. So, I took that step of faith and asked with my most sincere and desperate heart to be filled with the Holy Spirit. I can tell you there was nothing spectacular about that simple prayer the moment I said it other than a flood of peace and assurance that I had not had before. After

that prayer, however, when I continued on with my books, the Word and prayer, something was different. I had been filled with the Holy Spirit and began speaking in tongues.

I ask you to seek God for your own personal revelation in this area, but you must agree that something or Someone has brought you to this point. Here's what I suggest:

- Get still before God. Sit in silence for a few moments to quiet your spirit.
- Open your ears to the same inward voice of the Holy Spirit you received in measure when you were born again.
- Meditate on Jesus' post-resurrection words in Acts 1:5: "For John truly baptized with water, but you shall be baptized with the Holy Spirit not many days from now" (Acts 1:5).

Now pray the words below (or other words as God is leading you). Remember that we need to persevere in prayer (see Col. 4:2).

PRAYER CONFESSION

Holy Spirit, I'm ready to be filled with You completely, and that includes speaking in my heavenly language. I surrender to You completely and let go of any preconceived ideas and teachings I have had about the gift of tongues. You're the same Holy Spirit that came that day on Pentecost, and I want that same gift of tongues that fell over those believers that day. I lay all my fear and misgivings at Your feet in exchange for every gift You long for me to have. I need Your power to live a victorious life. I need You to show me how to pray God's will and direction about things my soul and body know nothing about. I want more of You more than anything. I'm desperate for You. I'm hungry for You. Please fill me with Yourself with the evidence of speaking in other tongues. Give me utterance. And now by faith, I receive the baptism in the Holy Spirit. It belongs to me in Jesus' name (see Mark 11:24). Amen.

If you prayed that prayer, then kudos! You have just been filled with God's power. You may feel as the reader above did and not be doing cartwheels, but things have drastically changed in heaven. Now run with it. Expect more. Press in. As you discover ways to utilize the Holy Spirit's power—especially in your prayer life—your life will dramatically change.

6

Helping to Do Life

And I will pray the Father, and He will give you another Helper,
that He may abide with you forever.
JOHN 14:16

A vibrant, personal, victorious, joyful relationship with the Holy Spirit often eludes typical Christians because they keep Him at arm's length. They assume that this third Person of the Trinity—who has always been and always will be, who has seen and been a part of it all, and who is the very mind of God—has little time or interest in the things that affect ordinary people like you and me.

Perhaps my favorite way to view the Holy Spirit comes from Jesus' own words: "And I will pray the Father, and He will give you another Helper, that He may abide with you forever" (John 14:16). The Holy Spirit is our Helper. He is there to help us do life! We call plumbers to help us with water pipe repairs, housekeepers to help us maintain our home and babysitters to help us with our kids. But the Holy Spirit? Can He really help us too?

Most certainly, yes! The words are right there in John 14:16. He is our *parakletos*, our Helper. The Paraclete is defined as "a strengthening presence, One who upholds those appealing for assistance."

Those appealing for assistance included two siblings I recently spoke to who have learned this truth firsthand. I asked these sisters separately to share an example of what the Holy Spirit has meant in their lives. Immediately, one particular and dramatic incident came to mind that involved them both. Here is what each of them wrote to describe what occurred:

Elaine's Story

Months before the ordeal happened, I had a dream that my sister Marie was at work, where a man took her hostage. I knew he was going to kill her. Our family all prayed diligently about that dream in every way we could think of, to cover all bases.

Several months later, I was at work when Marie called and said that she couldn't talk, but she didn't want me to worry when I heard about it on the news. She was okay and would call me later. I asked what she was talking about, and she said, "Do you remember your dream about me? It happened today."

Marie's Story

I became a correctional officer in February 1995. In May 1997, I had a dream that I was working in a large building on the prison complex that was unfamiliar to me. I heard the radio dispatcher say that the inmates were protesting. As I walked out of the building, the inmate who was leading the protest yelled my name and said, "Let's take her as a hostage!" My dream then turned to my mom standing in front of my casket, reading my obituary and talking about how unnatural it is for her child to die before her.

I awoke in tears, completely freaked. Then in a loud but loving voice I heard, "First Corinthians 3:23." I opened my Bible to that verse, which reads: "And you belong to Christ, and Christ belongs to God" (*NLT*).

In June 2000, I was transferred to a 32,000 sq. ft. building where I supervised 36 male inmates. Shortly after, Elaine called me and told me about her dream and insisted it was from the Holy Spirit. Our family began to pray for God's protection.

October 26, 2000, started out like any other day. I got
to work before picking up the inmates. As I was standing
in the tool room, conducting inventory, I felt the need to
pray. So I said, "Holy Spirit, I give You this day. Please have
Your perfect will. Lead me and guide me. Protect me; protect those around me. Give me wisdom." I finished my tool
inventory and picked up the 32 inmates who would work
for me that day.

Later, I walked into a small engraving room where four
inmate engravers were working. I looked at an inmate's
changes on the computer and acknowledged one correc-
tion had been made, but the other had not. As I was speaking to the inmate who had made the changes, another
inmate came up behind me. He grabbed me in a choke
hold with his right hand and held a shank (homemade
knife) to my neck with his left hand as he said, "Don't let
this turn into a murder."

I backed away, reaching for my pepper spray, but he
came at me harder and more desperately. He put the shank
to my throat once again, but this time, I could feel the sting
from the cut over my carotid artery. He repeated what he
had already said to me: "Don't let this turn into a murder."
I looked into his black, deadened eyes. At that moment, I
knew he had no regard for my life. My first instinct was to
cry, but then a peace washed over me. The inmates pro-
ceeded to take my keys, radio, pepper spray and handcuffs
from my duty belt and handcuffed me to a chair.

Immediately, I began reasoning with the two inmates
who were involved in the escape attempt. One of them
looked at me with his black eyes, pale face and red lips
dripping with saliva. He said, "I am serving three consec-
utive life sentences; I have nothing to lose by trying this or
by killing you." He put duct tape over my mouth. Suddenly, another inmate helped to free me after he overheard
the others talking about raping me. Soon tactical teams
arrived, stormed the compound and retook the prisoners.

I was held hostage for only 38 minutes. But other than some superficial injuries, including some bruising and a small cut on my neck, no one (including the other inmates) was hurt in the process. Through our dreams and the intercession of the Holy Spirit, no doubt God not only saved my life that day, but countless others as well. The Holy Spirit is the special mark of God's ownership on me!

He Is What He Is

I realize that Elaine's and Marie's stories of this hostage ordeal, and the warnings they received about it ahead of time, do not reflect the normal, everyday, run-of-the-mill, I-need-a-good-parking-space event. But I guarantee you that both of them have developed absolute certainty of the Holy Spirit's interest and willingness in helping them do life. They appealed for His assistance, and He provided it.

Asking for a parking space, however, is just as valid. As a matter of fact, it serves as an example of a lesser challenge we can practice trusting Him for so we'll be ready for the really big ones when they come. When I began my doctoral program, I was a single mom with three children (ages one, three and five). I bought a parking pass the first quarter but found it inconvenient and expensive. So, because every single minute and dollar of my life as a single mom was spoken for, I spent the next two-and-a-half years praying daily for parking spaces, and I found one every time! Many would argue that that was a silly misuse of the Holy Spirit, but my need was greater than any argument against it. He loves me, and the fact that I needed, believed and asked for those parking spaces validated my prayer. I appealed for parking assistance, and He gave it.

Through this and other similar experiences, I discovered that His strength was made perfect in my weaknesses (see 2 Cor. 12:9-10), and that I could even be thankful for those times when I couldn't accomplish something alone and needed the Holy Spirit to help me. Some days when I awoke, my sufficiency was at 80 percent; other days it was only at 20 percent. But if His strength was made perfect in my weakness, no matter what I did or did not have, His provision kicked in. Either way, I was always at 100 percent. In everything, I was always more than a conqueror (see Rom. 8:37). In everything I would always be okay. Why? Because He is what He is. He is my Helper who is present to help me for the big life-and-death issues as well as the small parking-space-finding needs.

So, if He is what He is, what exactly does it mean that the Holy Spirit is *your* Helper? What do His roles, functions, duties and obligations involve in your life?

He Will Become What You Allow Him to Be

I am technologically challenged. Computers, cell phones, Internet, social networking—none of their inner workings come naturally to me. I just don't think that way. I even called my son Clint once when he was in college to see if I needed to rewind a DVD! To compensate for my inadequacies, I have adopted as my strategy to just learn the basics (enough to get me by) and find others to help me with the rest.

Recently, I bought a new computer with all the bells and whistles. It's what I needed for all the future books I would write, right? Turns out the bells serve no purpose unless you ring them and whistles do no good unless you blow them. As a result, so far my computer has been reduced to a cheap, stripped-down generic version, and all the extra features have remained untapped. I still just know the basics, enough to get me by, and everything else gets lost on me—until Clint comes to our home and shows me something new. It's then I say, "Wow, I didn't know I could do that!"

For far too long, God's people have been living their lives with only the basics of the Holy Spirit. They don't know they can do anything through Him and that He is available to them with all the bells and whistles heaven can provide. But because they don't realize and utilize these benefits, the Holy Spirit is reduced to a cheap, stripped-down generic version of the Trinity. The fact is, He doesn't come with a manual containing a list of every feature that describes Him and every feat He can perform. Why? Because He waits for you to develop a relationship with Him so He can reveal Himself to you and personalize specific, unique ways He can help you.

Yes, He is what He is, but He also waits to become everything you will allow Him to be.

Take another look at John 14:16: "And I will pray the Father, and He will give you another Helper [Comforter], that He may abide with you forever." Knowing the meanings of a couple of the words in this verse will help clarify its meaning:

- *Another:* One besides; another of the same kind.
- *Helper:* One called alongside to help; one extending the ministry of Jesus to the end of the age.

In paraphrasing this verse, Jesus is describing the Helper as "One beside Me and in addition to Me, but one just like Me. He will do in My absence what I would do if I were physically present with you." In other words, the Holy Spirit is available to finish in your life everything that Jesus started in His. And when did Jesus tell you He would leave you? Never. Even when you mess up, the Holy Spirit doesn't run off.

Those who tell you that the Holy Spirit doesn't assist in finding parking places have probably never asked Him to help them do so. We have not, because we ask not (see Jas. 4:2). I can already hear some of you saying, "Yes, but asking for a parking place is asking 'amiss, that you may spend it on your pleasures' [Jas. 4:3]." If that's true, why does the *Amplified Version* of John 14:16 not only fail to limit the role of the Helper but also expand it to include more of those things we can need and even want?

> And I will ask the Father, and He will give you another Comforter (Counselor, Helper, Intercessor, Advocate, Strengthener, and Standby), that He may remain with you forever.

How are *these* roles defined?

- *Comforter:* One who consoles, soothes in sorrow, provides ease and quiet enjoyment; one who is compassionate, understanding, listens well, relieves someone from distress.

- *Counselor:* One who teaches, mentors, gives advice.
- *Intercessor:* One who mediates, pleads on the behalf of someone else.
- *Advocate:* One who takes another's side, represents the interests of someone else.
- *Strengthener:* One who fortifies, makes strong, toughens, makes resistant to damage, gives power to resist attack.
- *Standby:* One who is alert, dependable and stands ready.

The Holy Spirit becomes something for everyone. Jesus asked, the Father answered and the Holy Spirit came to cover every base. Kind of sounds too good to be true, as if I told you that someone had promised to leave you a large inheritance. Before you could count on what that person had to give, however, you'd want to know who that person was and what he was like. *Until* you did, you wouldn't feel as if you could completely trust that person or ask him for assistance. After all, a person's promise is only as valid as the integrity that stands behind it.

I am, in fact, delivering good news to you that Jesus left you a large inheritance. His name is the Holy Spirit; and everything He has to offer you is valid right now—yours for the taking. Do you need a comforter, counselor, intercessor, advocate, strengthener or standby? You can spend what He offers today. And integrity? He's oozing with it. And that comes out in who He is and what He does in individual lives.

Who He Is

Remember learning about "personification" in English class? You know, it's where human traits get assigned to non-living objects, such as a window winking or a diamond becoming a woman's best friend. Neither is possible, but both help to clarify the identities of those objects being described.

Personification naturally occurs in our search to discover who the Holy Spirit is, but this time, the Object is real and the descriptions are truly possible. He's not a power or force, and He is especially not an it! Jesus referred to Him as a "He":

> When He, the Spirit of truth, has come, He will guide you
> into all truth; for He will not speak on His own authority,
> but whatever He hears He will speak; and He will tell you
> things to come (John 16:13).

The Holy Spirit is a real Person. His personification continues
as we realize that He has a mind, will and intellect (see Rom. 8:26-
27). He speaks (see Rev. 2:7). He teaches (see John 14:26).

He can also be lied to (see Acts 5:3-4, *AMP*) and insulted (see
Heb. 10:29, *AMP*). He can be grieved (see Eph. 4:30), resisted (see
Acts 7:51) and quenched (see 1 Thess. 5:19). In addition, He can be
blasphemed when someone knowingly and willingly discounts the
work of the Holy Spirit (see Mark 3:29; Matt. 12:31-32). At the
same time, He forgives those who blaspheme without being aware
of what they're doing (see 1 Tim. 1:13).

I don't know about you, but these and other qualities give the
Holy Spirit a face to me. It makes Him personal. It provides what
I need to talk to Him as a trusted Friend. I can cry to Him when
I'm sad, and laugh when I'm happy. I can go to Him for advice,
and feel okay when I make mistakes. He is the real, tangible, approachable, always available, never wrong, forever trustworthy
member of the Trinity who takes pride in you spending your life-
time getting to know Him more.

What He Does

The word "Spirit"—or even more so, "Ghost"—can throw us off
course in our journey of getting to know Him in a greater way. He
is not some nebulous, spooky figure. The word translated "Spirit"
or "Ghost" in the New Testament is the Greek word *pneuma,* and
it means "breath, breeze, current of air, wind." That's why Jesus
said, "The wind blows where it wishes, and you hear the sound of
it, but cannot tell where it comes from and where it goes. So is
everyone who is born of the Spirit" (John 3:8).

Nadia was born of the Spirit in 1982, at age 19. In February 1997, she traveled from Ohio to Colorado to undergo a supposedly simple outpatient laparoscopic surgery; so she made the trip alone, without her husband. But from the beginning, the procedure went badly. They had trouble starting an IV. When they inserted a port in her chest, she felt intense pain. Because of her sedation, however, she couldn't speak to let them know not to continue the surgery. All she could do was pray silently. She came out of recovery and learned that they had punctured her spleen. Instead of four small portholes, the doctor had to cut her open from under her breastbone to her navel. He fixed the spleen, but Nadia lost a lot of blood and her lungs absorbed massive amounts of fluid.

Nadia and I had been close friends since I had lived in Ohio. One day, I called before I went to visit her at the hospital to ask what I could bring. She requested a CD player and praise music, and Nadia began entering into days and days of nonstop worship. Here's how she described it:

> For three weeks, I remained in the Holy Spirit's presence, cheek to cheek with my Savior through the Holy Spirit. The only time I would lower the music was when the staff needed to talk to me. I remember a housekeeper named Melvin who came to clean my room. He said, "Nadia, there is something so weird about your room. Every time I open your door, a warm, strong wind comes over me and goes 'Shoooosh.'"

What was the purpose of this presence of the Holy Spirit? Was He just there to provide a feel-good experience? After all, Nadia's condition continued to worsen. She ran a high fever, didn't sleep soundly and couldn't breathe properly because of the fluid in her lungs. She recalls crying out to God to spare her life so she could serve Him and finish raising her children. One night, she asked Him to give her sweet sleep without fear of dying. Her description of that event brought it all back to me as if it happened last week:

As I dozed off, I felt a strong slap on the left side of my upper back that awakened me. I fell back to sleep. Again I felt a strong and forceful slap—this time on my right upper back. The experience continued for what seemed like an hour, dozing off, getting slapped awake on the left then the right then the left then the right. I recall naming my angels Seraphim and Cherubim as I pleaded, "Stop, let me sleep!" Suddenly, several nurses and staff rushed into my room and forced me to wake up and walk so I wouldn't go into a coma or die.

The medical staff went on to work hard on Nadia. They issued a blood transfusion and eventually returned her soaring temperature and elevated heartbeat to normal, but it was the wind of the Holy Spirit that kept Nadia alive that night.

The Holy Spirit shows up everywhere, in every part of life. He's the muscle of God. He's the go-to part of the Trinity. He's the One who gets the process rolling. God gives the command in heaven, and the Holy Spirit makes it happen on earth. Every time you see God's power manifested, the Holy Spirit is on the scene. God said, "Let there be light!" and the Spirit kicked into gear and slung the universe into being. God said, "Save my daughter Nadia," and the Spirit did just that. He was just waiting to take action and manifest God's will and word into the natural realm. The wind blows where it wishes.

That same Spirit who kicked into high gear for Nadia that night also draws us to Christ, convicts us of sin, enables us to accept Christ as our personal Savior, assures us of salvation, and helps us live the victorious life.

Then the Holy Spirit goes on to help us understand Scripture. And who better to do that than He? After all, He wrote all the books of the Bible through the hands of individual men (see Rev. 1:19). In addition, He spoke through these people and prophesied through them. Then He didn't just let things be. He's the One who brings the Word (that He has written) alive so it doesn't just remain type on a page. He's the One who fulfills the prophecies spoken by the men whom He anointed to do the prophesying.

He's both the originator and the completer of the process. Everywhere you turn, there He is. Again, the wind blows where it wishes.

We've already seen how He helps us pray according to God's will (see Rom. 8:26-27,34; 1 Cor. 14:2-3,13-14). Our spirit prays to God's Spirit, and we know what God wants as a result. He also shows us how to effectively share Christ with others. He provides revelation (see 1 Cor. 2:9-10) and makes the supernatural possible (see Acts 1:8; 10:38).

I could go on and on about what all the Holy Spirit can and will do. As a matter of fact, I've struggled a bit with how to give Him adequate coverage regarding His roles, duties, functions and obligations.

But as I studied one and then another and then another of His characteristics, I realized that the descriptions were endless. Further, to attempt making a self-proclaimed exhaustive list and then failing to include something you need from Him today may do you a grave disservice. It could discourage you and keep you from accessing His provision in your area of need.

I similarly wrestled with finding just the right testimonies to illustrate comprehensively and appropriately different ways that women I have heard from have found the Holy Spirit faithful in the many helping areas of their lives. But the stories I received were all over the map. I found it impossible to organize them in any effective way.

Suddenly I realized that the challenges I faced were also indicative of a glorious truth. Yes, He is what He is described to be in Scripture, but He also becomes all that each of us needs Him to become whenever needs arise. I began to look at the Holy Spirit not only as the Helper, but also as the fill-in-the-blank Helper, the etc. Helper, the Helper forever saying, "May I help you?" He's our personalized Assistant, ready and waiting and willing to help us do life, whatever that involves. He's the one-size-fits-every-need One who dares you to start depending on Him for your very life.

Know Your Inheritance

Recently, I read that there is an estimated $60 to $400 billion in unclaimed inheritance money across the United States. If I told you today that your name was on the list of those who had an inheritance coming to you, wouldn't you find your way to the courthouse tomorrow? Why not claim your rightful spiritual inheritance through the Holy Spirit today?

If Elaine and Marie hadn't known their inheritance included Holy Spirit warnings about impending dangers, they would have totally missed out, and who knows what would have been the result. If I hadn't known that my inheritance included things as minor as finding parking spaces maybe 300 times during the remaining quarters of my doctoral program, I would have been stuck with the alternatives that belonged to everyone else.

There's an even greater truth hidden in this fact, however. Elaine and Marie didn't just wake up one morning with big hostage-taking victory levels of faith. They, no doubt, practiced on it first with the seemingly insignificant issues. Asking for help from the Holy Spirit for small thing after small thing and watching Him come through—that's the very thing that builds your faith. It's what creates a lifestyle of trusting in God. As a matter of fact, you simply cannot lift the heavy faith for mega-problems when they arise such as Marie's or Nadia's unless you've *been* lifting the smaller weights of faith over a prolonged period of time. You must build up to trusting God for the big things. Marie and Nadia had cultivated a lifestyle of faith through trusting God for the small things long before they encountered their desperate emergencies.

Last night, as it was getting dark, I went running with my dog, Murphy. He was feeling a bit frisky and took off. I've run this path many times with him, but this was the first time he'd disappeared. Murphy was gone for about 30 minutes. I began to think about the highway nearby and the mountain lions recently spotted in the area. I ran back to my car and drove up and down the street calling for him, to no avail. I began to wonder what I would do when it was totally dark and . . . then I stopped and prayed instead. "Holy Spirit," I said, "would You cause Murphy to turn around right now from where He is and head back to me?"

About two minutes passed, and here came Murphy, running as fast as he could toward his aggravated master. "*Bad* dog," I said. Then I looked up smiling and said, "*Good* Holy Spirit."

In the economy of heaven, does my dog matter? No way; but *I* do. And because of my ask-and-then-receive history with God, I know right where to go when the seemingly insurmountable things hit. Learning to depend on Him for the small things makes me automatically default to faith when the bigger issues arise. Through it all, I have come to realize that nothing that lies ahead can overtake me, and in everything I encounter, God is faithful.

He is what He is . . . and He's just waiting to become all that I will allow Him to be.

---

*M*ake It Yours
Let Him Help You Do Life

The Holy Spirit is the very representation of love, and He comes by it honestly. God so loved you that He sent His Son. Write out John 3:16.

_____

_____

_____

_____

_____

Jesus so loved you that He gave His life. Write out Galatians 2:20.

_____

_____

_____

_____

_____

The Holy Spirit so loved you that He came to reveal Jesus and His love to you. Write out Romans 15:30.

_____

_____

_____

_____

Now read 1 Corinthians 13:4-8. List what love *is* and what love *is not*:

_____

_____

_____

_____

What does this information in 1 Corinthians 13 tell you about what the Holy Spirit is, given that He is the very representation of this love?

_____

_____

_____

_____

Describe one or two areas in your life in which you need an extra measure of love where you find it the hardest to give. Then go back to the ways you just described the love aspects of the Holy Spirit and list the ways He will be sufficient in your insufficiency (see 2 Cor. 12:9-10).

_____

_____

_____

Take another look at the following roles, functions and duties that the Holy Spirit provides:

• *Comforter:* One who consoles, soothes in sorrow, provides ease and quiet enjoyment; One who is compassionate, understanding, listens well, relieves someone from distress.

- *Counselor:* One who teaches, mentors, gives advice.
- *Intercessor:* One who mediates, pleads on behalf of someone else.
- *Advocate:* One who takes another's side, represents the interests of someone else.
- *Strengthener:* One who fortifies, makes strong, toughens, makes resistant to damage, gives power to resist attack.
- *Standby:* One who is alert, dependable and stands ready.

What is one example of when the Holy Spirit performed one or more of these functions in your life?

_____

_____

_____

_____

What is an example of when He was at work in one or more of these ways, but where you didn't recognize Him?

_____

_____

_____

_____

What is an example of a time you faced difficulties but failed to call on Him for His help in specific areas?

_____

_____

_____

_____

The Holy Spirit is your Helper. Where do you need Him most to help you today?

_____

_____

_____

_____

Review the following list of the activities of the Holy Spirit. For each item, write out some ways in which you can now see that He was at work in your life in these areas.

Drawing you to Christ

_____

_____

_____

_____

Convicting you of sin

_____

_____

_____

Enabling you to accept Christ as your personal Savior

_____

_____

_____

_____

Assuring you of salvation

_____

_____

_____

Empowering you to live a victorious life

_____

_____

_____

_____

Helping you understand the Bible

_____

_____

_____

Guiding you in the way you should go

_____

_____

_____

Showing you how to pray according to God's will (see Rom. 8:26-27,34; 1 Cor. 14:2-3,13-14)

_____

_____

_____

Preparing and leading you into ministry (see Num. 11:17,25; John 1:33-34)

_____

_____

_____

Leading you to effectively share Christ with others

_____

_____

_____

Providing supernatural revelation (see 1 Cor. 2:9-10)

_____

_____

_____

Accomplishing the miraculous (see Acts 1:8; Acts 10:38)

_____

_____

_____

Other

_____

_____

_____

What is the greatest need in your life today? Describe it in detail.

_____

_____

_____

Given the information you have just described, how might you call on the Holy Spirit to be your Helper in this area?

_____

_____

_____

PRAYER CONFESSION

Holy Spirit, thank You that You are my Helper—not just other people's Helper, but my Helper. Thank You that You are waiting for me to ask and trust You in every single area of my life. Thank You that You are as interested in the small things as You are the big, scary things and even use the smaller, everyday things to build my faith. Thank You that there is no end to who You can and will be for me. Thank You for becoming personal to me. Thank You that I am learning that I can automatically call on You for help no matter what I face. And thank You, O Holy Spirit, for all You are teaching me today. In Jesus' name, amen.

$\mathcal{Y}$our Power and Authority

The heaven, even the heavens, are the LORD's;
but the earth He has given to the children of men.
PSALM 115:16

During World War II, a huge advertising campaign took place to encourage people to buy Series E war bonds from the U.S. Treasury. Marketed in the beginning as defense bonds and later as war bonds, the first certificate was purchased by President Franklin D. Roosevelt. Eighty million Americans bought at least one of these bonds. But the owners had to hold on to them until they matured 40 years later. As a result, many were never cashed due to being lost or the owner passing away. Today, more than $16 billion worth of the bonds remain unclaimed.

About the same time in our history as the bonds were being sold, a revival involving divine healing began and lasted until about 1958. My parents got in on that movement as you read in chapter 3, when my 18-year-old aunt was healed of a terminal condition. Dad and Mom went on to raise their eight children to expect the supernatural as the normal way of life for the child of God.

They got plenty of opportunities to watch that happen. I was born with a heart defect. I was almost five years old when my mother was told that I would not live to start school. Of course, these words devastated Mom some four years after God had healed her sister. She tried to wrap her mind around the fact that she would bury her second-born child at a young age. *But wait,* she thought. *Why does it say in Isaiah 54:13, "All your children shall be taught by the LORD, and great shall be the peace of your children"?*

Mom was young in her faith—young enough to believe the promises she read and that what God said was true. So instead of preparing for me to die, she prepared for me to live. She went out and bought my school clothes. I started kindergarten as a weak and sickly child who sat in the corner unable to participate in many of the activities of the other children. Slowly, however, I began to get better. By the end of first grade, I won a physical fitness award. I went on to become one of the biggest tomboys in my family. And today, more than 50 years later, I still enjoy a totally healthy heart. Hiking, biking, skiing and running remain my favorite pastimes.

No doubt my parents would have buried me if they'd believed only the doctor's words and failed to believe God's Word. But they *did* believe, and that made all the difference. Unlike those bond-holders who failed to cash in on what rightfully belonged to them, Mom recognized the power she had through the Holy Spirit, and she cashed it in. She proved the validity of God's promises that time, and many times that would follow.

I recently flew back to Ohio for my 40-year high school class reunion. We "re-uned," as Dave says. Some observers from that time in our lives thought that my family and I were strange because church responsibilities took us away from normal school activities. One person I saw that reunion weekend reminded me in a not-so-positive way about how Mom and Dad trusted God to heal my sister's broken arm instead of taking her to the doctor. As I listened to him criticize the approach they had taken, it would have been easy to agree that what my parents did was not so wise. It would have made me seem like everyone else.

But as the man spoke the words, I realized I *wasn't* like everyone else. We were miles ahead in what we had seen—God's power on display. So I took a stand. Instead of distancing myself from my past, I embraced, defended and acknowledged how proud I was that Mom and Dad had the faith and courage to trust God for the impossible. That trust did not involve an either-or choice. There were times they went to doctors, and there were times they gave God a chance to come through. Yes, that kind of gutsy faith would involve some miscues, but the more they trusted, the bigger the miracles grew. God was only limited by the constraints we imposed. And any day of the week, I would rather err on the side of trusting. After all, it's the provision that God made for us since time began.

The Original "Power to the People"

In Genesis 1:26-38, God gave Adam unconditional authority over the earth. It was called dominion. To "have dominion" means "to govern, rule, control, manage, lead, affect, impact." Human beings were made to carry out their governing, ruling and reigning responsibilities on earth. For that delegated authority to work well, two things were needed: good communication between heaven and earth, and power to perform the required functions. That's why the Holy Spirit was given to us.

"Then God said, 'Let Us make man in Our image, according to Our likeness; let them have dominion over the fish of the sea, over the birds of the air, and over the cattle, over all the earth and over every creeping thing that creeps on the earth'" (Gen. 1:26). God told His dominion-appointed created man to multiply and "subdue," or dominate, every other created thing. Then God gave him all the plants and animals to use and enjoy, and God saw that "it was very good" (Gen. 1:31).

The Fall altered, but did not cancel out, that rulership. Man's assignment to dominate everything on the earth still existed, but sin kept him from accomplishing what he had been created to do. More Old Testament verses followed, however, to remind man of God's original intent:

The heaven, even the heavens, are the LORD's but the earth
He has given to the children of men (Ps. 115:16).

And . . .

What is man that You are mindful of him, and the son of
man that You visit him? For You have made him a little
lower than the angels, and You have crowned him with
glory and honor. You have made him to have dominion
over the works of Your hands; You have put all things under his feet (Ps. 8:4-6).

In the Old Testament, we don't see widespread use of man's
God-given power and dominion. As we've already seen, supernatural enablement occurred only temporarily, for certain people to
accomplish specific tasks.

It was the Holy Spirit's arrival in the New Testament that
made the difference once again, however. He arrived on the scene,
and the great power handoff was underway (see Luke 24:46-49;
Acts 1:4-8; 2:1-11). First, Jesus received *His* power:

The Spirit of the LORD is upon Me, because He has anointed
Me (Luke 4:18-19).

Then the disciples received *their* power:

Then He called His twelve disciples together and gave
them power and authority over all demons, and to cure
diseases. He sent them to preach the kingdom of God and
to heal the sick (Luke 9:1-2).

Then we received *our* power:

And Jesus came and spoke to them, saying, "All authority
has been given to Me in heaven and on earth. Go therefore . . ." (Matt. 28:18-19).

Note that this is not someday power, but *today* power. Spiritual
power is the privilege of every believer who seeks to be filled to
overflowing with the presence of the Holy Spirit. We aren't born
again into God's Kingdom just to make it to heaven. We have been

reclaimed for our assignment here on earth—ruling, reigning and dominion-taking. And Jesus didn't just give to us God's power that He had received, but He told us that what we would accomplish would be even more spectacular:

> Most assuredly, I say to you, he who believes in Me, the works that I do he will do also; and greater works than these he will do, because I go to My Father (John 14:12).

Imagine! Greater than healing and casting out demons and raising the dead. Are we doing the *works* of Jesus, much less *greater* works than He did?

Dunamis and *Exousia* Plus

Though I saw how my parents capitalized on God's power, I have had to learn the process on my own (and am still learning). Sometimes I've done well at it, sometimes not so well.

One Wednesday when my kids were young, I had a really sick headache. I had to pull over on my way to children's church to throw up. I dropped them off, then moved my car to a corner of the parking lot. I leaned back against the headrest and prayed for myself for the first time. Before the words were out of my mouth, pop! My headache and nausea were gone. Suddenly I realized that I didn't have my healing earlier because I hadn't *asked* for my healing earlier (see Jas. 4:2).

You and I must start small and be more deliberate about seeking out opportunities to pray for ourselves and others. We don't just wait for some power explosion to demonstrate our power. It became ours when we were filled with the Holy Spirit; but the proof happens only when we put it to work.

Miracles and the supernatural should be the normal way of life for you and me. Though it may continue not to happen in our churches, we can make it happen in our everyday lives. When we see a need in ourselves, or others, we speak to the problem, commanding things to change and sticking with it until it does. We go to nursing homes or hospitals or to the residences of sick friends, and we practice putting to work what we read in God's Word. After all, we have all the power and authority of heaven backing us up.

There are four "power" words used in the New Testament. The first two are *ischuros* and *kratos,* both of which deal more with physical strength. But the Holy Spirit-given powers that Jesus received, then the disciples received, and then you and I received—which enabled us to accomplish the miraculous—were something different:

- *dunamis* power—the force, strength, ability, might and energy to influence circumstances. It's the "to be able" power.
- *exousia* power—the delegated authority to use *dunamis* power.

Dunamis power is God's ability imparted into us; it's the power that makes us able to accomplish miraculous things. *Exousia* power gives us the right to do so, and the name of Jesus becomes the *exousia* authority that brings about the results.

But the Holy Spirit didn't stop there. He didn't want the power gift He brought to lie dormant like the still-in-the-package-strength-promising exercise DVD one of my children gave me for Christmas several years ago. The Holy Spirit provided the power and authority, then He injected us with the needed *boldness* to put it to use:

Now when *they saw the boldness* of Peter and John, and perceived that they were uneducated and untrained men, they marveled. *And they realized that they had been with Jesus. . . .* Being let go, [Peter and John] went to their own companions and reported all that the chief priests and elders had said to them. So when they heard that, they raised their voice to God with one accord and said . . . "Now, Lord, look on their threats, and grant to Your servants that *with all boldness* they may speak Your word, by stretching out Your hand to heal, and that signs and wonders may be done through the name of Your holy Servant Jesus." And when they had prayed, the place where they were assembled together was shaken; and they were all filled with the Holy Spirit, and they spoke the word of God *with boldness* (Acts 4:13,23-24,29-31, emphasis added).

Boldness here is the word *parrhesia,* and it means "outspokenness; unreserved utterance; freedom of speech with frankness, candor, cheerful courage." This kind of boldness causes us to step out and put to use that which we possess. It's the opposite of cowardice, timidity or fear that marked the disciples' lives before Pentecost. *Parrhesia* is a divine enablement that comes to ordinary people like you and me so that we can exhibit spiritual power and authority.

It's not enough to possess money because of our family name; we've got to use it or it does no good. The same is true with our *dunamis* and *exousia.* It's not enough to *have* it; we've also got to *use* it—and it's the Spirit-given boldness that pushes us to do that. Look around. What needs do you see? They are the perfect practicing ground for putting your power to work.

When we were filled with the Holy Spirit, we received the three-pronged power gift: the *force* to accomplish the miraculous, the *authority* to accomplish the miraculous, and the *boldness* to accomplish the miraculous. Jesus told His disciples to do it:

And when He had called His twelve disciples to Him, He gave them power over unclean spirits, to cast them out, and to heal all kinds of sickness and all kinds of disease. . . . These twelve Jesus sent out and commanded them, saying . . . "Heal the sick, cleanse the lepers, raise the dead, cast out devils. Freely you have received, freely give" (Matt. 10:1,5,8).

Jesus told the 70 disciples to do the same, as recorded in Luke 10:9. Then, with His last words, He told you and me to do it before ascending to heaven:

Go into all the world and preach the gospel to every creature. . . . And these signs will follow those who believe: In
My name they will cast out demons; they will speak with
new tongues; they will take up serpents; and if they drink
anything deadly, it will by no means hurt them; they will lay
hands on the sick, and they will recover (Mark 16:15,17-18).

The *dunamis, exousia* and *parrhesia* had extended the delivering
rule of the kingdom of God over hell's works and human hurts to
Jesus, and then to the disciples and to us. The Spirit-empowered
dunamis gave us the force and ability we needed. The Spirit-empowered *exousia* gave us the authority we needed. And the Spirit-
empowered *parrhesia* boldness gave us the courage we needed to
get the job done. All we have to do is boldly speak to the storm.
We get to dominate and have dominion. We get to put the devil on
the run. So what are we waiting for?

Balance of Power

Before we go out and change our world with our newly discovered
power, we need to be able to counter at least two arguments
against what we're doing. Both are good things, but they are applied incorrectly and prevent the very power Jesus told us to use.
They are God's sovereignty and God's will.

"God, if it be Your will, heal this person."

"God, You are sovereign and will do what you want, but please
heal this person."

We must be careful not to use these prayers as convenient, explainable backups in case God doesn't come through. Sovereignty
means "superior to all others; supreme in power, rank and authority." Indeed, God *is* sovereign; He does have the last word. But if
we leave everything miraculous up to Him, it relieves us of any responsibility for utilizing our faith.

God's sovereignty must be balanced with our duties. Neglect
of this balance can produce apathy or irresponsible attitudes. We
are responsible and accountable for what happens on earth. Earth's

problems are ours, and we are assigned to be the agents for their solution. The ball is in our court. The world literally stands or falls based on the actions and stewardship of human beings. And the victory our world and the people in it face is impacted by *our* stewardship, not someone else's!

When Joshua needed to take down Jericho, God said, "Do something! Start marching!" The duties weren't left to God or someone else with a bigger name. Joshua and the Israelites had to take charge.

I once attended a new bank opening with my dad. One of the festivities included handing out keys at the door to give visitors the opportunity to unlock a chest full of money. If that happened, that winner could keep all the change her hand could scoop out.

I was just a kid, so I prayed, "God, let Dad get the right key." But he didn't, and *I* did. My key opened the lock, and I filled my hand as full as I could and treated everyone in my family at the local Dairy Queen.

Too often, we forget that *we* hold the key to victory for the needs we face. We think, *If I can just get so-and-so to pray.* We assume that *other* people are the ones who have the power. But all along, you and I hold the same key as every other born-again, Spirit-filled believer, and we are just as able to get the job done. We can speak to every problem and command things to change!

Through the Holy Spirit, we've all been made partners with God in reestablishing His rule over circumstances and situations on earth. Adam's fall damaged the original partnership between man and God, but redemption set the recovery in motion. The arrival of the Holy Spirit made it complete, and we could once again have dominion—rule, subdue, reign, have power and take authority over—anytime, anywhere, for anything.

Just realize that God does little—if anything—on this earth without our cooperation (see Ps. 8:6). He doesn't just butt into our affairs whenever He wants. Instead, He defers to the dominion and authority He assigned to us. Until Jesus comes back, God will confine His activity on earth to our requests. His movement is triggered and brought about by you and me. We're the ones responsible for causing Him to act. Prayer and faith are the catalysts for making that happen.

The prayer we need to remember when seeking God's will in any given situation is this: "Your kingdom come. Your will be done on earth as it is in heaven" (Matt. 6:10). God's will is anything that belongs in heaven. Does sickness belong there? Will we find poverty or depression there? No way. If something isn't welcome in heaven, it's not welcome in God's kingdom among His people. That's how we know how to pray His will. In Matthew 8, the New Testament chapter where the miracles of Jesus are first recorded, one man came to Jesus and said, "Lord, if You are willing, You can make me clean" (v. 2). Jesus' answer was simple and straightforward: "I am willing; be cleansed" (v. 3).

He wants us to use the boldness that He has given us (see Heb. 4:16) to accomplish through the power that He has also given us. Be specific. Tell Him what you want. Ask big. Practice often. He's willing. Watch as the big, sovereign God who is in partnership with you does *big* things.

> Ask, and it will be given to you; seek, and you will find; knock, and it will be opened to you. For everyone who asks receives, and he who seeks finds, and to him who knocks it will be opened (Matt. 7:7-8).

Satan Behind Every Corner

There is one more huge misconception in the Body of Christ that de-powers us and keeps us from accomplishing the miraculous. It involves the works of Satan. Some see Satan behind every corner, while others don't see him at work in *any* situation. Many of us are taught that we can't talk directly to Satan, but instead should talk to Jesus *about* him. That's like trying to discipline a child from the next room.

No one taught Paul to do that. A demon-possessed girl kept following him, and it really started to get on his nerves. So, through the boldness the Holy Spirit had given him, Paul used his *dunamis* and *exousia* to speak directly to the demon and command it to leave. And it did (see Acts 16:18)!

We have to give Satan permission before he can do anything in our lives. That's why he buffaloes us through his lies and deceptions. He wants us to think we have no power over him. He wants us not to recognize when he's at work. And he definitely doesn't want us to know we have power over him and can speak directly to him. But he's not to be feared; he's to be recognized and resisted head-on.

Many years ago, my parents' pastor in Arizona was out in the desert one day and came across a giant diamondback rattlesnake. He killed it and cut off its head for life-threatening reasons. While the man carried the snake back to his truck, it continued to shake its rattler and lunge at him. And this pastor relayed how he continued to flinch even though he knew the snake's head was cut off.

That's the way we often react to Satan. He was defeated and his head was cut off at Calvary, so we don't need to flinch or be intimidated by him. Further, we need to recognize that he comes to kill, steal and destroy, while only Jesus brings abundant life (see John 10:10). Guess what? If what you're facing isn't bringing abundant life, you can be sure Satan is at work somewhere behind the scenes. Too many times we attribute some of the difficult circumstances we're facing to other people or situations. While we're busy assigning blame, Satan is getting off scot-free!

So do as Paul did: Command Satan, in the name of Jesus, to get lost. If he sticks around, do it again and again until he knows that *you* know.

Is your child sick? Is your marriage on the rocks? Are your finances a shambles? Let the she-bear come out in you (see Prov. 17:12). We all know to run far away when a mother bear starts protecting her cubs. Let's do the same. Let Satan know you mean business. Not in my house you won't! You can't have my child! I won't let you destroy my marriage! Let's wise up, face up and speak up—and keep speaking up—when it comes to overcoming the one who has already been overcome.

Recognize Your Power

When my son, Clint, was eight years old, we moved to Colorado Springs so that I could go to work for Focus on the Family. I'd been a single mom Clint's whole life, so he had seen more than his share of difficulties in a single-parent family. Perhaps as a result, Clint had a problem with his explosive temper that sometimes frightened his two sisters.

One day, it happened again. Clint "lost it" on the girls. He ended his tirade with a simple explanation: "I can't help it, I just get my temper from . . ." and he went on to name a certain family member.

That was it! I still had too much of my mom (and the she-bear) in me to hear a statement like that. I said, "Oh no, you don't, Son, sit down!" I guided him to a couch in our piano room and began to set him straight. O. J. Simpson's murder trial was taking place at that time and was dominating the news. I said, "Clint, let's just say that O. J. *is* guilty. He didn't wake up that day with his out-of-control temper. He had it when he was 3 years old, and 8 and 12—and no one took care of it."

I reminded Clint that he had asked Jesus to come live in his heart when he was in kindergarten, and then I asked him, "Do you think that kind of anger belongs in the same place where Jesus lives?"

We sat on the couch that day and took authority over this scourge in Clint's life. It was a simple but confident and frozen-forever-in-our-hearts prayer.

Sometime later, Clint came to my room one night where I was reading on my bed. He said, "Mom, I have a problem. I have to write a paper in my Bible class [he attended a Christian school] about the last time I lost my temper, and I don't remember when that was."

What a joyous moment this mom had of reminding her son about what God had done that day—when we did business on something that did not belong in his life—through the power of God just waiting to be put to work from inside of us.

The results of that experience didn't end there. When Clint was 21, I headed to the airport one cold December day to pick him up from the airport for Christmas break from college. I knew that he had gone to see that angry family member the night before and had once again witnessed the same results. I remember right where we were on the interstate as Clint, now six-foot-four, cried and relayed to me the ordeal that had taken place after he'd tried to talk about Jesus to that person, and the rage that had resulted. Clint said, "I am so thankful for what Jesus did for me that day. If we hadn't gotten hold of *my* anger, I would have taken it into my future marriage and passed it on to the children I will have someday."

Last week, 24-year-old Clint, still free from anger, asked for Sarah's hand in marriage. They are planning a late spring wedding next year; and with everything in me, I am honored to release my fine son to take a wife. Sarah is not getting someone who will explode and fly off the handle, as once could have been the case. Instead, she is marrying one of the finest human beings (even apart from being his mom) that I have ever known. And why is that the case? We cashed in our war bonds. We recognized our power. We realized and took authority over something that didn't belong in his life.

As for me, while I write these words, I remember about a generation following Joshua's that wasn't quite so blessed:

> When all that generation [Joshua's] had been gathered to their fathers, another generation arose after them who did not know the LORD nor the work which He had done for Israel (Judg. 2:10).

It's too late to tell me God doesn't do miracles anymore. I learned from my mother what rightfully belonged to me, and then I practiced for myself and passed it on to my son. He will discover it for *himself* and pass it on to the children he and Sarah will have. The next generation *will* know what happened on the couch that day when two people recognized the power and authority and boldness they had in Christ.

What an incredible and victorious way to live life!

Make It Yours
More Power to You

Read the following two Bible stories and then answer the questions that follow:

> And behold, two blind men sitting by the road, when they heard that Jesus was passing by, cried out, saying, "Have mercy on us, O Lord, Son of David!" Then the multitude warned them that they should be quiet; but they cried out all the more, saying, "Have mercy on us, O Lord, Son of David!" So Jesus stood still and called them, and said, "What do you want Me to do for you?" They said to Him, "Lord, that our eyes may be opened." So Jesus had compassion and touched their eyes. And immediately their eyes received sight, and they followed Him (Matt. 20:30-35).

> Now they came to Jericho. As He went out of Jericho with His disciples and a great multitude, blind Bartimaeus, the son of Timaeus, sat by the road begging. And when he heard that it was Jesus of Nazareth, he began to cry out and say, "Jesus, Son of David, have mercy on me!" Then many warned him to be quiet; but he cried out all the more, "Son of David, have mercy on me!" So Jesus stood still and commanded him to be called. Then they called the blind man, saying to him, "Be of good cheer. Rise, He is calling you." And throwing aside his garment, he rose and came to Jesus. So Jesus answered and said to him, "What do you want Me to do for you?" The blind man said to Him, "Rabboni, that I may receive my sight." Then Jesus said to him, "Go your way; your faith has made you well." And immediately he received his sight and followed Jesus on the road (Mark 10:46-52).

Do you think the two blind men and Bartimaeus recognized that they had power? Why or why not?

_____

_____

_____

How did they acknowledge the authority they had to ask for help? Who was that authority?

_____

_____

_____

What indication was there of the boldness they found to ask Jesus for help?

_____

_____

_____

_____

What did Jesus tell them to do?

_____

_____

_____

What did Jesus do as a result?

_____

_____

_____

_____

What is a serious problem that you or someone you know is facing right now? What *dunamis* power has been given to you over that problem?

_____

_____

_____

What *exousia* authority do you have?

_____

_____

_____

_____

What *parrhesia* boldness do you have the right to exercise?

_____

_____

_____

_____

What do you want God to do for you or that person? Be specific.

_____

_____

_____

_____

What is keeping you from getting the job done?

_____

_____

_____

_____

In Luke 5:12-13, we read, "And it happened when [Jesus] was in a certain city, that behold, a man who was full of leprosy saw Jesus; and he fell on his face and implored Him, saying, 'Lord, if You are willing, You can make me clean.' Then He put out His hand and touched him, saying, 'I am willing; be cleansed.' Immediately the leprosy left him." What does this story say about whether or not it was God's will to heal this man?

_____

_____

_____

What is the rule we talked about earlier in the chapter for always knowing God's will?

_____

_____

_____

_____

_____

What does this story tell you about whether or not it is God's will to answer your prayer?

_____

_____

_____

What do you now know that you didn't know before reading this chapter, and what difference will it make in your life?

_____

_____

_____

_____

_____

PRAYER CONFESSION

Holy Spirit, thank You for the gift of dunamis *power and* exousia *authority. They are gifts that empower me to accomplish the miraculous anytime for anything for anyone. Thank You for* parrhesia *boldness that is also a gift from You. I could not do what I am supposed to do without Your enablement. But You gave me the ability to accomplish, the right to accomplish and the boldness to accomplish. And now I will accomplish. I will never again allow Satan to intimidate me. I will ask, and it will be given to me. I will seek and find. I will knock, and the door will be opened. Thank You. Amen.*

$\mathcal{H}$e Builds Character

But the fruit of the Spirit is love, joy, peace, longsuffering, gentleness,
goodness, faith, meekness, temperance: against such there is no law.
GALATIANS 5:22-23, *KJV*

I helped teach a large Sunday School class once at a church we attended in Cincinnati. My children and I also assisted with the church's inner-city ministry where we physically and spiritually fed the homeless.

One Sunday morning as class was about to convene, a young woman stood from where she was sitting in the second row. She asked if she could say something. I, like many others, immediately locked my eyes onto her hair. The length was just below her shoulders, and the color was two-toned. The first several inches from the roots were black and the rest was platinum blond.

My attention was quickly averted, however, to the words the woman spoke. She told us that she was a new believer and had helped with the inner-city ministry the day before. While witnessing to someone on the street, she made an immature judgment and lit up a cigarette with the man she was talking to. Immediately, one of the ministry leaders ran out of the building, jerked the cigarette from her mouth, stomped it on the ground and berated her in front of the stranger as he turned and walked away.

Then the woman faced all of us so we could see her head-on. She pointed to her hair and said it represented her spiritual growth so far. She touched her black roots and explained that they represented the drugs and alcohol she had conquered. Then she pointed to her blonde ends and said, "This is where I still need to grow. Please be patient with me."

I still remember where I sat and where this nameless woman stood as she pointed out a lesson to me that I will never forget: Showing love is the most important thing. But this is the area where we often fumble. We wear ourselves out doing ministry while neglecting more crucial matters. I have lived and worked in secular arenas as well as Christian ones, but conflicts, strife and generally less-than-loving responses among God's people have become a major inhibitor to accomplishing His Kingdom work in these last days. Whether at home, in women's ministry or at work, we don't have to look far to see that we're not doing well in the area of loving others and being patient and kind and forgiving toward one another. In many cases, this contention has cost us our health, prosperity, ministry and especially our effective witness, as it did with the woman who spoke that day. How can we ever be a light to the world when we can't even get along with each other and stay focused on such unimportant things? I witnessed some of these problems even as a child.

One Sunday when I was about 12, I was baptized in the creek near our church. When I came back to the car, I was putting on my shoes with my right hand and holding on to a car with my left. While doing so, someone closed the car door on my left pinkie finger. The rest of the day, my bandaged, smashed finger continued to throb with every beat of my heart. Later that afternoon, I was sitting in the back of our church when one of the older women came inside. She walked over and looked at me with concerned eyes. I was in bad need of sympathy, so I was glad she stopped by. But my comfort was short-lived when she said, "Honey, don't you think you should get out of church while you are wearing those shorts?"

The Bible teaches that love and its associated characteristics should always be our default response as we strive to be more like Christ; but all too often, the goal evades us. Peace, kindness, gentleness and grace don't come naturally, no matter how long we have walked with God—especially for us ladies. Take a look at these verses:

> Better to dwell in a corner of a housetop, than in a house shared with a contentious woman (Prov. 25:24).

> Better to dwell in the wilderness, than with a contentious and angry woman (Prov. 21:19).

> A nagging wife is as annoying as the constant dripping on a rainy day. Trying to stop her complaints is like trying to stop the wind or hold something with greased hands (Prov. 27:15-16, *NLT*).

We girls are really good at expecting others to do things our way. We also excel at keeping track of wrongs. Then when the slightest next event occurs, all the previous infractions converge, and we blast with both barrels. It reminds me of the charcoal briquettes I once thought were cold, so I placed them in my metal garbage can on the curb in front of my apartment. Soon, from my second-story window, I saw smoke billowing from the can. The embers had reignited with the first winds that blew.

Such is the case with conflict: We assume we've forgiven or forgotten, then a slight wind blows, and the events come back in vivid detail. In Joyce Meyer's book *Life Without Strife*, she writes about what this seemingly harmless and common response within the Body of Christ really looks like. She describes a man who attended her conference for many years who had a vision following a heated argument he had with his wife. Joyce wrote:

> In a vision, the man saw a large, fierce demon spirit wearing heavy armor. The man could see each piece of the armor and understand its symbolic meaning. The spirit wore the helmet of PRIDE and the breastplate of UNRIGHTEOUSNESS. He carried a sword of BITTERNESS and a shield of HATRED. From his belt hung a hammer of JUDGMENT. He wore a cloak of DECEPTION, and his

feet were shod with boots of ANGER. He entered, SPEAK-
ING FORTH LIES.[1]

We've all encountered strife. It's one thing, however, to have
experienced strife, but quite another to see its source as Satan, and
his goal as destroying and distracting everything good that you
are working toward. Ridding yourself of anything but loving responses to others is for *your* sake and the resultant impact on the
works of God, and less for the sake of the other people involved.
Like you, I have *been* the victim and *done* the victimizing when it
comes to strife and contention. But there is no room for it *anywhere* in the kingdom of God. And little else can move forward or
grow or make its maximum impact until this battle is won. It's
ours for the winning, because of the Holy Spirit living inside us.

First Things First

One of my favorite quotes comes from C. S. Lewis: "You can't get
second things by putting them first. You get second things only by
putting first things first. Put first things first and we get second
things thrown in. Put second things first, and we lose both first
and second things."[2]

We all want to jump right in and start doing the ministry God
has called us to do. But as this quote tells us, we'll never be effective in the real work until the necessary prep work is complete. I'm
not the world's best painter, because I want to go ahead and start
painting before the stripping, sanding and cleaning are done. Any
painting results will never be effective until I learn to put first
things first.

This truth is demonstrated back in Exodus 39. The passage
talks about the high priest. No one can argue that his work wasn't
important. He served as mediator between God and the people.
When someone needed something from heaven, his or her only re-
course was to go through this provision on earth. But before the
high priest ever began his work, God instructed Moses about the
dress code required. Here is what his robe would look like:

And he made the robe of the ephod of woven work, all of blue. And there was an hole in the midst of the robe, as the hole of an habergeon, with a band round about the hole, that it should not rend. And they made upon the hems of the robe pomegranates of blue, and purple, and scarlet, and twined linen. And they made bells of pure gold, and put the bells between the pomegranates upon the hem of the robe, round about between the pomegranates; A bell and a pomegranate, a bell and a pomegranate, round about the hem of the robe to minister in; as the LORD commanded Moses (Exod. 39:22-26, *KJV*).

Your eyes might be glazing over right now as you wonder what in the world an ancient priest's robe has to do with a chapter on the fruit of the Spirit, but hang in there with me. This is pretty amazing stuff.

On the hem of the priest's blue robe would hang alternating bells and pomegranates. The pomegranates acted as pads between hand-beaten gold bells that chimed together in perfect harmony. Worshipers knew what the priest was doing and which way he was turning by which bell was emitting its purity of sound. Without these fruits, the bells would have clanged together in chaotic discord.

Now go in your Bible to 1 Corinthians 12 and 14, where the Holy Spirit gives gifts to God's people. In between those chapters, however, comes chapter 13, which talks about the importance of love. Look at the first three verses:

Though I speak with the tongues of men and of angels, and have not charity [love], I am become as sounding brass, or a tinkling cymbal. And though I have the gift of prophecy, and understand all mysteries, and all knowledge; and though I have all faith, so that I could remove mountains, and have not charity [love], I am nothing. And though I bestow all my goods to feed the poor, and though I give my body to be burned, and have not charity [love], it profiteth me nothing (1 Cor. 13:1-3, *KJV*).

Many Bible scholars have drawn a correlation between the Exodus 39 description of the high priest's robe and these 1 Corinthians 13 verses. Just as the pomegranate fruit kept the bells on the robe from clanging against each other, love and the fruit of the Spirit interspersed regularly between the gifts of the Spirit make them work most effectively. These three verses bring the point home in an incredible way. They say that no matter how talented you are, if you don't demonstrate love, you'll be ineffective. Regardless of your vast gifts, if you don't allow patience and kindness and forgiveness to permeate your very existence, the success of your outreach will never come to what we might call "fruit-i-tion."

We will discuss the gifts of the Spirit in chapter 9, as well as how to fulfill our purpose in chapter 10. But before we can ever successfully launch out in those areas, we *must* do adequate prep work. Otherwise, we'll all be a bunch of talented (but loveless) people clanging our gifts against each other in a cacophony of noise rather than a smooth-running, harmonious, working-together Body of Christ. We *must* put first things first, and those first things are contained in the fruit of the Spirit. Once we master those, we get a bunch of second things thrown in.

So let me help you lift the second-things desires in your life to the shelf for a while as we tackle first things. Let me help you conquer the love thing.

Choosing the Spirit Walk

Isaiah talked about the arrival of the Holy Spirit and how that would affect the "fruit" areas of our lives:

> Until the spirit be poured upon us from on high, and the wilderness be a fruitful field, and the fruitful field be counted for a forest (Isa. 32:15, *KJV*).

Before the Holy Spirit was poured upon us, we were on our own in trying to change our character. What we saw is what we got. But *when* the Holy Spirit arrived, you and I received the provision and the ability to become a fruitful field. The New Testament details what this fruitful field would be like:

> But the fruit of the Spirit is love, joy, peace, longsuffering, gentleness, goodness, faith, meekness, temperance: against such there is no law (Gal. 5:22-23).

Fruit (*karpos*) describes "that which is produced by the inherent energy of a living organism." If we've discovered anything about the Holy Spirit inside us so far, it's that He's very much alive; He's a living organism.

The alternative is discussed at the beginning part of this same chapter. It details what happens when we chose to walk in the flesh (adultery, fornication, uncleanness, lasciviousness, idolatry, witchcraft, hatred, variance, emulations, wrath, strife, sedition, heresies, envy, murder, drunkenness, reveling, and the like). From adultery to strife, idolatry to envying, murder to hatred. It's amazing how we often consider only the "big" sins, but God lumps them all together. Here you learn that when you take part in strife and contention, you are caving in to the flesh. Once again, instead of living from the inside out, you're settling for living from the outside in. And it all keeps you distracted from the exciting and fulfilling road forward. But then, enter the Holy Spirit:

> Walk in the Spirit, and you shall not fulfill the lust of the flesh (Gal. 5:16).

Walking in the Spirit means to be "occupied with or engaged in." It means walking along the path that God lays down. As you walk in the Spirit, He talks to you, guides you, tells you what you should or should not do and how you should respond. You grow in Christ as you increase your resistance to everything that is uncharacteristic of Him. Walking in the Spirit allows you to stop memorizing rules and start obeying based on the Holy Spirit's leading within you. You do freely what is right—not because God's law tells you to. Pretty neat arrangement, huh?

A lady wrote an article for me once in my magazine. She'd endured a difficult divorce, and the court had determined among other things that the children would spend Christmas day with both parents. They tried it that way at first, but this mother was bothered by the inconvenience and disruption the children experienced. So though it was her right to see them, she let go of her court right and chose to walk that higher, heavenly, Spirit-led road. She relinquished her time with her children on Christmas day and announced a new celebration with them, which she called "Second-Sunday Christmas." They started meeting with members of her family on the second Sunday in December, and it became a great tradition from then on. The woman closed with these words: "When I made it right for my kids, God made it right for me, too."

You see, holding on to our rights is not what walking in the Spirit means. The fact that you *can* say or do or respond some way doesn't mean you *should*. Walking in the Spirit means you're walking to the beat of a different drummer called the Holy Spirit. That often means that you let go of your pride, lay down your rights, keep your mouth closed and move to the back seat. Walking in the Spirit means you're keeping your eyes glued on eternal things, and the tiffs you're tempted to get involved in aren't a part of that journey. In the process, I've learned time and again that God often changes the situation—and often the other person—by changing me. The conflict is resolved when I lay down my weapons and take up the fruit. Amazing how that works!

The power of the flesh is broken as the power of the Holy Spirit is allowed to produce the fruit of the Spirit in you. And what is this fruit? Though "fruit" is singular, it consists of nine separate parts. I see it like a large Harry-and-David fruit basket. Though called a fruit basket, it contains many different kinds of fruits. And to receive one means you gain the benefit and nourishment and enjoyment of them all! The same is true with the fruit of the Spirit.

The Fruit

When you are about to receive that Harry-and-David fruit basket, you're given a description of all the scrumptious fruit that are coming your way. With the fruit of the Spirit, you receive love, joy, peace, longsuffering, gentleness, goodness, faith, meekness and temperance. Let's take a closer look at these nine delicious, God-characteristic fruits you will receive.

Love (*Agape:* Unconditional Affection, Benevolence)

Agape love is the foundational quality of the fruit of the Spirit and happens as we abide in the true Vine. It is uniquely different from the other three kinds of love:

1. *Eros.* Takes. It's a physical love.
2. *Epithumia.* Takes. It's an attraction, puppy love.
3. *Phileo.* Gives and takes. It's a reciprocal love between friends.

Agape gives. It's that unconditional love that meets the needs of others. Every word for "love"/"charity" found in 1 Corinthians 13 is the Greek word *agape*. We can find no better definition of that *agape* love than in the passage itself. Love *is* patient, kind. It *does not* envy, boast, keep record of wrong or delight in evil, but rejoices in truth. It *is not* proud, rude, self-seeking or easily angered. It *always* protects, trusts, hopes and perseveres. And we find that *agape* love never fails. It will never run out, prove false or be in vain.

When Jesus asked Peter three times if he loved Him (see John 21:15-17), Peter assured Him that he did. What Peter didn't realize, however, was that *agape* was an option. The verb he used was *phileo,* which as we saw above meant a friendship kind of love. Friendship is good, but Jesus offered something better. Peter finally realized his love option had just expanded to include the unconditional *agape* love feast. He discovered the very love of God resident inside him and available to be given out. The same is true for you and me (see John 13:34-35).

Joy (*Chara*: Cheerfulness, Delight, Gladness)

Remember how Isaiah prophesied that when the Holy Spirit would be poured upon us, we would become a fruitful field and counted for a forest? Joy plays a role in that process and is contagious in the way it affects others. As the psalmist states, "Let the field be joyful, and all that is in it. Then all the trees of the woods will rejoice" (Ps. 96:12).

We want the world to want what we have, and that invitation becomes most appealing when we demonstrate joy—joy that remains even when the diagnosis is bad; joy that cannot be shaken; joy that becomes our very strength (see Neh. 8:10). The author and source of that inexhaustible joy available to us is the Holy Spirit (see Acts 13:52; Rom. 15:13; 1 Thess. 1:6).

Peace (*Eirene*: Peace of Mind, Tranquility)

Peace passes all understanding (see Phil. 4:7). My friend Nora recently told me about the unsaved lesbian woman she worked for who asked how she seemed so at peace when her father was dying and she was facing some grave problems with one of her children. Peace demonstrated through turmoil is one of the loudest witnesses to our faith. Peace is abundantly available to those walking according to the Spirit, but it remains out of reach to those walking in the flesh. Tell me that the Holy Spirit is not in hot pursuit of Nora's boss and using people like Nora to demonstrate His fruit in doing that (see Acts 9:31; Rom. 8:6; 14:17).

Longsuffering (*Makrothumia*: Patience, Perseverance, Bearing up Under)

Dave's first wife was chronically ill throughout their 32-year marriage. The fruit of *makrothumia* enabled him to endure. It's the quality of character that doesn't allow you to surrender to circumstances or succumb to trials. It also makes you patient when it comes to difficult people. This kind of longsuffering causes you to not only endure and bear up under difficult things, but also to be grounded in beneficial expectation. *Makrohtumia* is inspired by hope and mercy; and once again, its source is the Holy Spirit (see 2 Cor. 6:6).

Kindness (*Chrestotes:* Tender Concern for Others)

It's sometimes hard to remember that the fruit of kindness already belongs to you when someone puts you on hold or treats you rudely. But when you allow kindness to pervade your life every day and to permeate everything you do, you develop a genuine desire to treat others gently just as the Lord treats you. Harshness and austerity are exchanged for grace, a tender heart and a nurturing spirit (see 2 Cor. 6:6).

Goodness (*Agathosune:* Acting in a Manner for the Benefit of Others)

Christians showed up to help after Hurricane Katrina. Your church ministers to the homeless. You forgive and continue to do good things for someone who treats you wrong, and you don't expect anything in return. This character quality is more than being gentle, kind or mellow. It doesn't just *feel* good; it *does* good. It does something about it (see Eph. 5:9).

Faithfulness (*Pistis:* Firm Persuasion, Conviction, Belief in the Truth)

We can *think* we believe something or feel prone, compelled or even predisposed to being on board with something. But when we're persuaded, we're convinced, and nothing can ever "unconvince" us. Faith is the foundation of persuasion. Faith is the currency we use to transfer God's provision from the unseen realm to the natural, earthly realm. The Holy Spirit is the power behind your persuasion that allows you to believe, have faith "anyway." He enables you to believe no matter what (see Acts 6:5; 11:24; Gal. 5:5).

Gentleness (*Praotes:* Meekness, Humility)

Gentleness is that Holy Spirit sedative that diffuses tense situations. It's that thing that kicks into gear and refuses to allow you to get riled up. Nothing frustrates a contentious person more than to be met with gentleness. If we had more of *praotes* in our churches, we'd have a lot less strife. Gentleness is an always-win, never-lose, Spirit-inspired tool you can use to deal with difficult situations (see Gal. 6:1; 1 Pet. 3:4).

Self-control (*Egkrateia:* Continence, Temperance)
Self-control allows you to determine ahead of time what your limits will be and then function within those boundaries. Self-control enables you to master your desires and restrain your passions and appetites. The opposite is *akrasia,* which means excess and self-indulgence, and it leads to a person's demise. In Numbers 11:34, the Israelites buried the people who God had struck down because they yielded to their cravings at a place called Kibroth-Hattaavah.

Self-control keeps you anchored (see 1 Cor. 6:12). Self-control prevents you from being mastered, ruled by, brought under the power of, or in bondage to any person or emotion or object or addiction. Instead, you maintain authority and power over all those things. You stay in control. The key to self-control is the refusal to allow your enemies (flesh, world, Satan) to rule or hold you captive in any way. Self-control secures your freedom to love, maintain joy, experience peace, interact with patience, demonstrate a kind disposition, act out of goodness, live in faithfulness and respond with gentleness. Self-control as fruit of the Holy Spirit is the decision to live and remain within the boundaries of victory (see Gal. 5:24; Zech. 4:6).

The Image Emerges

A story is told about Renaissance sculptor Michelangelo when he was carving the David statue. The observer worried about how much marble Michelangelo wasted as he continued to create his masterpiece. But the artist's defense was simple: "As the chips fall away, the image emerges."

As the fruit grows bigger in you, the other stuff falls away and the image of Christ emerges. I used to think that I had to spend my whole life trying to achieve and grow into these seemingly unattainable fruit qualities. But the day I realized that love, joy, peace, patience and all the others already belong to me, I started taking advantage of them. I began to spend these fruits on the ordinary things in my life. I loved when I would have formerly sought revenge. I felt joy instead of fear and sorrow. Peace replaced anxiety, longsuffering replaced impatience, and kindness replaced grumpiness. In the process, I found myself seeking ways to demonstrate His goodness, exercise my faith, and build my life on self-control through the Holy Spirit.

The world teaches that it's all about you, and more, more, more becomes the mantra. God teaches that it's all about Him, and less, less, less of you becomes the goal. On the surface, it seems like a questionable choice, but in the end you discover it's the only way to go. By choosing first things, you get everything else thrown in. By giving yourself away, you gain everything that God is. And the more fruit the world sees in you, the more you look like the very image and reflection of Christ.

As for me, I will see Your face in righteousness; I shall be satisfied when I awake in Your likeness (Ps. 17:15).

The process of being formed in the likeness of Christ doesn't wait to happen until *then*. Instead, it began the moment you were filled with the Holy Spirit and His fruit became yours. It continues every day as you respond with more love, joy, peace, longsuffering, kindness, goodness, faithfulness, gentleness and self-control.

The fruit are yours for the taking right now in every situation in which you find yourself. Recognize them, claim them, use them and become them. And don't be satisfied ever again with anything less than one day walking in His likeness, and today bringing you one step closer through the fruit of His Spirit!

*M*ake It Yours
Allow Him to Give You His Character

One more time, here are the fruit of the Holy Spirit: love, joy, peace, longsuffering, kindness, goodness, faithfulness, gentleness and self-control. Go back into the chapter and review their meanings, and then answer the following questions:

Which of the fruit has intersected your life in the most memorable way? Tell about that event.

_____

_____

_____

_____

Which has most eluded you?

_____

_____

_____

Which of them do you need most in a situation that you are presently facing?

_____

_____

_____

_____

Post a list of all the fruit in your car, at work, on your refrigerator, beside your phone—any place that reminds you what your default responses should be.

How we conduct our relationships with other people is extremely important to God. And we are not meant to enjoy this fruit only by ourselves; we are also meant to give it away. The Bible shows us how to do that through all of its "one anothers." First, look up these "love one another" verses and note the quality each encourages.

John 13:34-35; 15:12

_____

_____

_____

Romans 13:8

_____

_____

_____

_____

1 John 4:7,11-12

_____

_____

_____

_____

1 Peter 4:8

_____

_____

_____

_____

Are you starting to get the message? We are to *love one another*—in our thoughts as well as our actions! From the seeds of that love, we are also to . . .

- *Be humble:* "If I then, your Lord and Teacher, have washed your feet, you also ought to wash one another's feet" (John 13:14).

- *Seek peace and harmony:* "But if you bite and devour one another, beware lest you be consumed by one another!" (Gal. 5:15).

- *Put others first:* "Be kindly affectionate to one another with brotherly love, in honor giving preference to one another" (Rom. 12:10).

- *Not judge:* "Therefore let us not judge one another anymore, but rather resolve this, not to put a stumbling block or a cause to fall in our brother's way" (Rom. 14:13; see also Jas. 4:11-12).

- *Build up others and edify them*: "Therefore let us pursue the things which make for peace and the things by which one may edify another" (Rom. 14:19).

- *Be gentle*: "With all lowliness and gentleness, with long-suffering, bearing with one another in love" (Eph. 4:2).

- *Be kind:* "And be kind to one another, tenderhearted, forgiving one another, even as God in Christ forgave you" (Eph. 4:32).

- *Comfort others:* "Therefore comfort each other and edify one another, just as you also are doing" (1 Thess. 5:11).

- *Serve others:* "For you, brethren, have been called to liberty; only do not use liberty as an opportunity for the flesh, but through love serve one another" (Gal. 5:13).

- *Forgive others:* "Bearing with one another, and forgiving one another, if anyone has a complaint against another; even as Christ forgave you, so you also must do" (Col. 3:13).

- *Pray for others:* "Confess your trespasses to one another, and pray for one another, that you may be healed. The effective, fervent prayer of a righteous man avails much" (Jas. 5:16).

- *Show compassion:* "Finally, all of you be of one mind, having compassion for one another; love as brothers, be tenderhearted, be courteous" (1 Pet. 3:8).

- *Be hospitable without complaining:* "Be hospitable to one another without grumbling" (1 Pet. 4:9).

And one last reminder to love one another, ladies:

And now I plead with you, lady, not as though I wrote a new commandment to you, but that which we have had from the beginning: that we love one another (2 John 1:5).

Why?

_____

_____

_____

_____

So we, being many, are one body in Christ, and individually members of one another (Rom. 12:5).

Sounds like a tall order, I know, but not if you start right where you are. Think about the most challenging person in your life. Choose two or three, if you like. Go back over the one-another verses above and write out your fruity-plan of response to that person(s) from this point forward, based on what these verses require. Be specific.

PRAYER CONFESSION

Glance back over the verses we've covered in this chapter, and then compose a prayer confession officially instituting the fruit of the Spirit in specific parts of your life.

Holy Spirit,

_____

_____

_____

_____

_____

_____

Amen.

Notes

1. Joyce Meyer, *Life Without Strife: How God Can Heal and Restore Troubled Relationships* (Lake Mary, FL: Charisma House, 2000), p. 2.
2. C. S. Lewis, *God in the Dock* (Grand Rapids, MI: Eerdmans, 1970), p. 280.

e Assigns Abilities

As each one has received a gift, minister it to one another,
as good stewards of the manifold grace of God.
1 PETER 4:10

I remember it well—"All-day's meeting with dinner on the ground." For real, that's what we called it. Members at Dad's church in rural Indiana knew to reserve the third Sunday in August every year for this event. Lots of preaching, singing and offering-taking took place on that day. But I'm not ashamed to admit, it wasn't the church service that lasted from about 11 A.M. to 3 P.M. that I looked forward to. No way. It was the dinner afterward. Wooden carpentry sawhorses were set in place across the lawn beside the church. Then long, flat boards were laid on top and covered with tablecloths, and when the service ended, the indulgence began.

Fried chicken, chicken and dumplings, chicken potpie. Meatloaf and ham. Fresh garden potatoes, corn, green beans and lettuce abounded. And the desserts? We often had to set out extra tables to showcase all the "sweets" that showed up. I remember my mother once baked 19 pies for a similar event.

I get hungry just thinking about the wonderful food we enjoyed on those days. What made it especially good was that people didn't just randomly contribute any ol' thing. Instead, everyone brought their *best* dish—their tried 'n' true, everyone-loves-and-expects-it, nobody-can-make-it-better dish. Every year, Allegra brought her tamales, Lucy brought her butterscotch brownies and Sherrie brought her German chocolate cake. The meal became an annual masterpiece of everyone's best. That's what made it so delectable and so complete.

Able-bodied

Well, it turns out the Bible sort of talks about the dinner aspect of our "all-day's meeting with dinner on the ground." It's called the Body ministry, and it's where people bring their best dishes (called gifts) for the meal served to the collection of believers (called the Church).

> For as the body is one and has many members, but all the members of that one body, being many, are one body, so also is Christ. For by one Spirit we were all baptized into one body. . . . For in fact the body is not one member but many (1 Cor. 12:12-14).

> For as we have many members in one body, but all the members do not have the same function, so we, being many, are one body in Christ, and individually members of one another (Rom. 12:4-5).

The Body of Christ is the church. It's the Greek word *ekklesia*, and it means "assembly"—assemblies of local groups of believers as well as assemblies of all believers in universal fellowship around the world. The job of the Church is to accomplish Jesus' work on the earth until He comes back. That enormous but doable task doesn't happen by just one or two or three people. Like the physical body that requires the coordinated work of all members—such as the eyes, ears and even nose hair, as well as those things you *can't* see, like the heart, lungs and kidneys—the Church requires the combined efforts of everyone. In the physical body, some of its parts are big (legs and arms), while other parts are small (fingernails and earlobes); and the same is true in the Church. But in both, each individual part is equally essential for the whole to function well. And when one body part fails to do what it is created to do, bad health results.

Think about all the different jobs it takes to pull off a week's worth of ministries at your local church and churches throughout the world. Some of those contributions people make are obvious and applauded while others take place behind the scenes. It's easy to desire the more appealing, visible, gratifying and affirming gifts and to observe a Beth Moore or a Nicole Mullen and envy *their* gifts. But such a mindset causes us to conclude that our own skill set is less important than are those up front. God knew we'd feel this way, so He addressed our emotions before we ever felt them (see 1 Cor. 12:15-25).

I once met a man named Jerry who attended our church in Cincinnati. He told about how he became a Christian. His wife of nearly 30 years had left him, and one Sunday morning, he made his way to church carrying all that was left of his belongings packed inside the trunk of his car. Desperate, rejected, lonely and sad, he walked toward the door of the church. Then a parking-lot attendant turned to him, looked him in the eyes and deposited much-needed love in Jerry's heart. "Hi, I'm Rudi," the attendant said. "Welcome."

Jerry described how he came back the next Sunday and the next. If Rudi's back was turned to him, Jerry said he would slow his steps so Rudi would see and speak to him again. Jerry eventually gave his life to Christ. But I ask you, whose job was more important: the pastor who preached the sermons, the person who prayed with Jerry to be born again, or Rudi who loved him and kept him coming back?

Every part of the Body of Christ performs a unique function essential to the Body as a whole, and God is holding us accountable for our faithfulness. When Rudi and the rest of us stand before Jesus, man's esteem, opinion and estimation of our gifting will no longer matter. Instead, our rewards will be based on how we cheerfully continued the work we were assigned in the process of bringing people like Jerry into the Kingdom and helping him grow in Christ.

As you effectively walk out your gift-fulfilling journey as an important part of the larger Body of Christ, you will find that when one member of that Body gets smashed or cut or splintered, the pain affects the rest of the Body too. This truth makes us rethink being the cause of anyone's hurt feelings or rejections (see 1 Cor. 12:26-27).

We also rejoice when others find their gifting fit. Dave and I are the proud parents of six children (four girls and two boys), four sons-in-laws, one almost-daughter-in-law and six grandchildren. Seldom is it possible for all of us to get together, so Christmas features varying configurations of attendees around the tree. One thing stays the same, however: All family members open gifts specifically chosen just for them. Angie often gets something to assist her great musical talents; Courtney enjoys cooking-related contributions to one of her favorite activities; and Nate gets his I-can-always-count-on-them Brooks Brothers, non-iron, slim-fit shirts to enhance his work wardrobe.

The most special gifts of all, however, are the ones that bring that I-knew-you-would-love-it smile from the giver's face. It shows just how involved that giver was in deciding which gift to give. It also shows how completely the giver knew the one receiving the gift.

The gifts you receive to serve the Body of Christ aren't haphazard, subjective or capricious. They have been thoroughly thought through and chosen before you were ever created. And if you could just see the I-knew-you-would-love-it smile from the Giver's face, you'd know just how involved He was in the gift He picked just for you, and how well He needed to know you to make it happen. And guess who that Giver is?

Triune Gift-Giving

Not one, but three Givers give gifts to us as believers—the Father, the Son and the Holy Spirit.[1] The input of all three reveals the importance of the task and the intense interest and activity invested by each member of the Trinity in providing you with the resources, encouragement and assistance you need to receive and fulfill your individual assignment.

Some of these three-sourced gifts sound similar to one another, but the numbers and variety of them reflect the vast differences in the ones who would receive them—you and me. *None* of the Godhead leaves us on our own to try to find meaning with our lives. *None* of them fails to be involved. *Each* of them does His part in keeping these job descriptions forever before us—as together they lovingly offer something for every one of us to uniquely accomplish with our lives.

Gifts from God the Father

The gifts from God the Father include prophecy, ministry, teaching, exhorting, giving, leading and showing mercy. How amazing to realize that the gifting you were born with originated with the One who originated everything else. Just as He created the earth and sea and sky to function just the right way, He created and equipped you with your unique assignment and every skill you would need to accomplish it:

> For as we have many members in one body, but all the members do not have the same function, so we, being many, are one body in Christ, and individually members of one another. Having then gifts differing according to the grace that is given to us, let us use them: if prophecy, let us prophesy in proportion to our faith; or ministry, let us use it in our ministering; he who teaches, in teaching; he who exhorts, in exhortation; he who gives, with liberality; he who leads, with diligence; he who shows mercy, with cheerfulness (Rom. 12:4-8).

You might have read the list and found your abilities spanning more than one of these categories. That's not unusual. Different aspects of several gifts can be present while only one trait is especially dominant. Keep that in mind as you explore the other gifts that are available.

Gifts from the Son

The gifts from the Son include apostles, prophets, evangelists, pastors and teachers. Scripture says that you and I are joint heirs with Jesus (see Rom. 8:17). That means He is our Brother. That means we are all part of the same family. That means we have a function to perform within that family unit. And that means that you and I must diligently accept and work within our given assignments right alongside Jesus:

> Therefore He says: "When He ascended on high, He led captivity captive, and gave gifts to men." . . . And He Himself gave some to be apostles, some prophets, some evangelists, and some pastors and teachers, for the equipping of the saints for the work of ministry, for the edifying of the body of Christ, till we all come to the unity of the faith and of the knowledge of the Son of God, to a perfect man, to the measure of the stature of the fullness of Christ . . . from whom the whole body, joined and knit together by what every joint supplies, according to the effective working by which every part does its share, causes growth of the body for the edifying of itself in love (Eph. 4:8,11-13,16).

These are sometimes called the "ministry offices" or "fivefold ministry." They are essential in making sure the gifts from the Father and the gifts from the Spirit are applied properly in the church. This Ephesians passage lists the office gifts and the reason they exist. As verse 12 tells us, the purpose of these Jesus-given gifts is for the "equipping of the saints." The word "equip" means "to prepare, train, perfect, make fully qualified for service" and "to recover wholeness as when a broken bone is set and needs to mend."

In other words, one person's gift is given to encourage the maturity (see v. 13), stability (see v. 14) and integrity (see v. 15) of other individual members of the Body. One of the main tasks of your pastor and women's ministry leader is to cultivate the individual and corporate ministries of those he or she leads. It results in the whole Body's growth and edification (internal strengthening). My gifting used properly helps you use your gifting properly so that you can help others use *their* gifting properly. Mature gifting becomes visible evidence of greater power and testimony, thereby edifying the Church and evangelizing the world around us.

Dave came to me one afternoon while I was writing this chapter. He'd received a call from a family member who works on staff at a large church. He had the unpleasant task of confronting someone who works under him, and he had requested that we pray with him about it. Ephesians 4 was still in the forefront of my mind. So, instead of stressing with and begging for this family member, I thanked God for the opportunity he had for using *his* gifts to help the other member of the Body become prepared, trained, perfected and made fully qualified for service through God's equipping-the-saints provision. Through this process, both got to perfect their gifts and make them most effective for the Body and the Kingdom at large.

Gifts from the Holy Spirit

The gifts from the Holy Spirit include the word of wisdom, word of knowledge, faith, gifts of healing, working of miracles, prophecy, discerning of spirits, tongues and interpretation of tongues. The Holy Spirit is also majorly involved in the area of gift assignment. As a matter of fact, 1 Corinthians 12, the Bible passage that describes the gifts of the Spirit, once again begins by listing the organized and coordinated teamwork of all *three* parts of the Trinity in working together to impart gifts to God's people: the same Spirit, the same Lord, and the same God who works all in all:

> There are diversities of gifts, but the same Spirit. There are differences of ministries, but the same Lord. And there are diversities of activities, but it is the same God who works all in all. But the manifestation of the Spirit is given to each one for the profit of all: for to one is given the word of wisdom through the Spirit, to another the word of knowledge through the same Spirit, to another faith by the same Spirit, to another gifts of healings by the same Spirit, to another the working of miracles, to another prophecy, to another

discerning of spirits, to another different kinds of tongues, to another the interpretation of tongues. But one and the same Spirit works all these things, distributing to each one individually as He wills (1 Cor. 12:4-11).

Paul identified a spiritual gift as a supernatural ability bestowed on an individual by the Holy Spirit, not as a heightened natural ability. Think about that. Every single gift in every single one of us is a fingerprint of the Holy Spirit, evidence of His personal activity in each of our lives. These gifts are available to every believer, and the Holy Spirit is the One who chooses who gets what (see 1 Cor. 12:11). Our job is to understand how we're gifted, and then we're to develop and put to use that gifting in the place where we are assigned (see 1 Cor. 13:1; 14:1).

The purpose of the Holy Spirit-given gifts as well as those provided through God the Father and God the Son is for the common good of the *entire* church. We are a whole Body made up of individual gifts—including yours and mine, much like a flower bouquet. We each bring our own color and fragrance to the Body alongside others doing the same. Your gift is meant to "profit" (v. 7) the Body of Christ. That means "to bring together, benefit, be advantageous to."

Spiritual gifts are not badges of honor or signs of spiritual maturity. They are also not earned; that's why they're called gifts. They are to be prayerfully recognized, gratefully accepted and faithfully developed and used. God the Father, the Son and the Holy Spirit make the assignment, and you fulfill it, and then they bring forth the increase! That's the process.

What's the Anointing Got to Do with It?

I once bought a dress for a convention that Dave and I would attend. Problem was, as soon as I arrived, I saw another woman wearing the identical dress, and I made my way back to my room to change before anyone else could see.

Though the list of the gifts we've talked about in this chapter is exhaustive, the ways the Holy Spirit develops them and lives them out in us is not. These gifts are not hanging like identical clothes on a rounder in a department store to be duplicated by every woman who takes them home. Though two people can be gifted teachers, they will both teach in different ways. Manifestations of the gifts are crafted around the uniqueness of the person assigned to them, and that's where the anointing comes in.

The correlation between the gifts you receive and the anointing you get to use them is evident. The Greek word used for "anointing" is *chrisma*, and the Greek word used for "gifts" is also *chrisma*. You receive *chrisma* to accomplish your *chrisma*.

The *meaning* of "anointing" is "ointment, something smeared on." The *purpose* of the anointing is to empower you to uniquely use your gifts and fulfill your calling supernaturally rather than merely out of your own intellect and ability. The *source and power* behind the anointing is the Holy Spirit. The *arrival* of the anointing on your life comes at the new-birth experience and at the called-and-separated-into-ministry experience.

When God chooses you for a particular ministry, He also anoints you. He gives you a job to do, and then He smears His super-charged, performance-enhancing ability over you to get it done. If you're called and anointed to work in administration within the Body, you'll not be an effective worship leader. On the other hand, when you're working within your gifted calling, the anointing ignites your work, and it becomes apparent to all. You were born with your anointing and it will be with you until you die: "For the gifts and the calling of God are irrevocable" (Rom. 11:29).

Paul acknowledged that his effectiveness in ministry did not come from his skills (see 1 Cor. 2:4). Even Jesus couldn't count on His human ability alone but relied, instead, on the anointing (see Luke 4:18).

That's why you need to recognize the role of the Holy Spirit's anointing on *your* gifts too. "But the anointing which you have received from Him abides in you, and you do not need that anyone teach you; but as the same anointing teaches you concerning all things, and is true, and is not a lie, and just as it has taught you, you will abide in Him" (1 John 2:27). The One who assigned you the gift will also anoint you to use it and even provide the places for you to plug it in. You don't have to make a place for yourself. The Holy Spirit delights in doing that for you.

My mother told me once about a dream she had while my dad was pastoring his church. In her dream, she saw Dad serving in an orchestra director-like role. He was helping everyone tune up their instruments so they could play a common song.

Several years ago, I studied the book of Haggai and the re-building of Solomon's temple. To get the people pumped up to do that, Scripture says that "the Lord stirred up the spirit of Zerubbabel" (Hag. 1:14). And guess what it means "to stir up"? It means "to arouse to action; to awaken musical instruments, get-ting them ready to play."

In the New Testament we read, "Therefore I remind you to stir up the gift of God which is in you through the laying on of my hands" (2 Tim. 1:6). Dad's gifts stirred up my gifts so that I could stir up yours. As I have written this chapter, I can almost see my-self with my baton lifted, tuning you all with your separate and wonderful instruments to eventually play a common song.

Working Faithfully Where We Have Been Called

Joni Eareckson Tada tells a story about a woman named "Mary Rose." One time, Joni was busy with last-minute preparations be-fore speaking before thousands at a convention. Joni writes, "The air behind the platform was heavy with importance." Suddenly, someone led Mary Rose, who was crippled with cerebral palsy, to Joni. Her escort explained that she had been waiting to meet Joni since she had read one of Joni's books decades earlier and how it had changed her life. Meanwhile, Joni was thinking, *Don't they know I'm trying to concentrate?* But Mary Rose smiled and said, "I've been praying . . . for you . . . every day . . . since I read your book." Joni's quick math told her that Mary Rose had prayed for her some 7,000 times, and her irritation evaporated. Then Mary asked to pray for Joni again before she spoke. She did, and then her es-cort led her away.

It was Joni's next words that I have never forgotten: "Mary Rose slipped silently into the shadows, while I wheeled out into the light. . . . I've already received a lot of my reward. . . . [but] the highest accolades will [someday] go to godly people who have labored loyally with no recognition. . . . In His eyes, there are no little people because there are no big people. . . . Success in ministry . . . is not the key. Faithfulness is."[2]

My life has been filled with people, like Tammy and Paula, who work behind the scenes in the places where they have been gifted. My life has also been filled with many well-known people who work up front in the places where *they* have been gifted. The goals for all of them are the same, however—to work faithfully where they've been called for the collective Body of Christ and to seek the approval of no one but God.

There was a time in my life when I put way too much stock in the people I knew and the fact that they knew me. I enjoyed the accolades I received for my work. But that had to change. Several years ago, God pulled me back. He had me stop speaking and writing books for a while, sit at His feet, learn from Him and get my priorities in order. He went to work perfecting me, changing me and teaching me that I am but one of His children specially chosen to do but part of the work for the Body of Christ. My job is to do it faithfully, without pride and for God's glory only. Unless and until I learned that lesson, my life and my work would never accomplish all it was intended to do.

This book is my first on this side of that perfecting process. You've seen glimpses of some of the consequences that have resulted in me thus far. The Holy Spirit continues to lovingly guide and teach me in more areas, but He and I know where I've come from, and I love Him more than ever because of it. That's why I had to write about His role in my life and ministry. I originally called this book *The Missing Piece,* because until I allowed Him to decrease me and increase Him, I wouldn't witness a fraction of all God longs to become in my life.

So for today's "dinner on the ground," I offer my best dish to the Body of Christ through my writing, as it joins with your gift and all the others to create the complete meal. George Ella Lyon wrote a children's book called *Together* that kind of sums it all up. Here's a portion of what she wrote:

> You cut the timber, and I'll build the house.
> You bring the cheese, and I'll fetch the mouse.
> You salt the ice, and I'll crank the cream.
> Let's put our heads together and dream the same dream.[3]

Though I don't know you personally, what an honor it is to lay my dish down beside yours. What an honor it is to stir up my gifts as I encourage you to stir up yours. And what an honor it is to put my head together with yours and dream the same dream.

---

*M*ake It Yours
Identify and Develop Your Gift in Your Body

Think about the many gifts you see operating in your church. Look again at the various Trinity gifts below and identify the area(s) where you've been gifted.

Gifts from the Father (see Rom. 12:4-8):

- *Giving prophecy:* Those who see life with prophetic insight or deliver public prophecy (see 1 Cor. 12:10).

- *Doing ministry:* Those whose special creation gifts enable them to effectively serve the Body in physical ways (see 1 Cor. 12:5).

- *Teaching:* Those who instruct the revealed truth of God's Word.

- *Exhorting:* Those who provide encouragement to the members of the Body.

- *Giving:* Those gifted to contribute to the emotional and/or physical support of others, or those gifted with abundant financial means to finance the work of the gospel.

- *Leading:* Those who are gifted to effectively facilitate, and those who work in administration.

- *Showing mercy:* Those gifted with strong perceptive emotions, and those called to Christian relief or acts of charity.

Gifts from the Son (see Eph. 4:8,11-16):

- *Apostles*: Those called to be a messenger or spokesperson for God to extend the work of the Church, open fields to the gospel and oversee larger sections of the Body of Jesus Christ.

- *Prophets*: Those called to be a spokesman/proclaimer with a special, divinely focused message to the Church or to the world. Those uniquely gifted at times with insight into future events.

- *Evangelists*: Those gifted to preach or witness in a way that brings unbelievers into the experience of salvation.

- *Pastors*: Those gifted to shepherd, nurture, teach and care for the spiritual needs of the Body.

- *Teachers*: Those gifted to impart knowledge.

Gifts from the Holy Spirit (see 1 Cor. 12:4-11):

- *Word of wisdom:* Spiritual utterance at given moments through the Spirit supernaturally disclosing the mind, purpose and will of God as it relates to a specific situation.

- *Word of knowledge:* Supernatural revelation of information relating to a person, event or particular purpose usually having to do with an immediate need.

- *Gift of faith:* A unique form of faith that goes beyond natural faith and saving faith. It supernaturally trusts and does not doubt with reference to the specific matters involved.

- *Gift of healings:* God supernaturally performs healings by the Spirit.

- *Working of miracles:* A divine enablement to do something that could not be done naturally.

- *Prophecy:* An edifying revelation of the Spirit for the moment. It involves insight of the Spirit and brings about exhortation or comfort on the part of the recipient.

- *Discerning of spirits:* The ability to view into the spirit world and to determine the source of situations or motives in people's lives.

- *Different kinds of tongues:* Speaking supernaturally in a language not known to the individual and is used mostly for private worship.

- *Interpretation of tongues:* The ability to share in a corporate setting the meaning of a public tongues message.

Now, with a different color of ink, go back over these gifts and name a specific person(s) you know who is gifted in each particular area. Write their names beside their gifts.

Go back over the gifts listed above again. What's left without a name beside it? Does that mean you don't see this gift at work in your church? For each unclaimed gift, write beside it "opportunity" or "people," depending on whether you think the absence is due to a lack of *opportunity* or to a lack of *people* gifted in that area.

Now look at the drawing of the Body on the following page. Use that diagram to represent the church Body of which you are a part, and then answer the questions that follow.

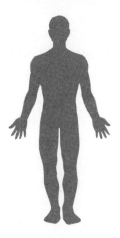

Who is represented by the head?

_____

_____

_____

Fill in your gifts and various people's gifts that you named above
at other places on the body. Once you spread out people's names
and gifting across the body, circle the one (excluding the head)
that is the most important, and put an *X* on the one that is least
important. Obviously, this is a trick request. Why are no gifts more
important than others? Why do you think God set it up this way?

_____

_____

_____

What does this all-gifts-are-equally-important truth tell you about
your place in your church Body and your commitment to fulfill it
in the days ahead?

_____

_____

_____

Read the parable of the talents in Matthew 25:14-30. Verse 14 says
that the Master "called his own servants and delivered his goods to

them." Who gave the talents to the servants? Who did we learn offers the gifts to us and decides what we get?

_____

_____

_____

Verse 15 tells us that the master gave talents "each according to his own ability." What does this tell you about the forethought and individualization that went into the gifts you have received?

_____

_____

_____

_____

What does this parable tell you about what happens when you use your gifts and abilities wisely?

_____

_____

_____

_____

What does this parable tell you about what happens when you neglect your gifts and abilities?

_____

_____

_____

_____

Sometimes it's hard to pin down where we are gifted and what God has called us to do. When it happened to Moses, God told him to simply look at what was in his hand (see Exod. 4:2). If this quandary describes you today, take a few minutes and sit quietly with a piece of paper or your journal in front of you. What situations or people particularly hold your interest or make you cry? In his book *Holy Ambition,* author Chip Ingram calls this your "dislocated heart."

If you know how you've been gifted but don't know where to put it right now, get to work on the thing that is right in front of you at the place where you are right now. Though it may not be a perfect match for your gifting, God places a lot of stock in faithfulness. Reread Matthew 25:21-23. What do those verses say to you?

_____

_____

_____

_____

_____

PRAYER CONFESSION

Holy Spirit, thank You that You join with God the Father and God the Son to give good gifts to us as believers. Thank You for the gifts You have given me and the ways You have lined things up in my life to put my talents to work. Thank You for this, another reminder, about what You've equipped this member of the Body to do as well as the wherewithal to do it. Thank You for opening the right doors for me to go through and for making Your instructions to me clear. In Jesus' name. Amen.

Notes

1. In 1 Corinthians 12:4-6, Paul makes it clear that the gifts of the Spirit are linked to all three members of the Trinity. Paul suggests that God the Father and Jesus Christ, God the Son, are involved alongside the Holy Spirit in distributing spiritual gifts. According to Dr. Gordon Fee, Paul regularly uses the term "Lord" to refer to Jesus Christ and the term "God" to refer to God the Father (see 1 Cor. 1:3; 8:6; 2 Cor. 13:14). For this reason, I believe that three Givers—the Father, Son and Holy Spirit—give these gifts to us. The input of all three reveals the importance of the task and the intense interest and activity invested by each member in providing us with the resources, encouragement and assistance we need to fulfill our individual assignment. (See Gordon Fee, *The First Epistle to the Corinthians* [Grand Rapids, MI: Eerdmans, 1987], p. 587 and notes 22-23.)
2. Joni Eareckson Tada, *Holiness in Hidden Places* (Nashville, TN: J. Countrymen, 1999), pp. 50-53.
3. George Ella Lyon, *Together* (New York: Orchard Books, 1989).

10

*H*e Enables You to Fulfill Your Purpose

May He grant you according to your heart's desire,
and fulfill all your purpose.
PSALM 20:4

I have spoken often through this book about my mother, who played a major role in my passion for Jesus. Throughout the years, people often asked her about the secret to her depth and acquaintance with the Lord, and she would always answer the same way: "I just fell in love with Him." As a teenager, I asked God for a double portion of what Mom had. I'd heard the sermon about how Elisha received his double portion from Elijah, so I felt free to do the same.

Over the past several years, Mom's health has declined, so I have flown back and forth between Colorado and Indiana to spend as much time with her as possible. While writing this book, I flew to see Mom for the final time. It became apparent that she would soon be with Jesus. My sisters and I decided it would be best to have someone stay with her at the nursing home 24/7, so I volunteered to take the night shifts. Early Wednesday morning, March 10, 2010, I pulled a chair close to her bed to talk to the same

One my mother had grown to love. I asked Him to pass me her mantle, an act also performed by Elijah to Elisha (see 1 Kings 19). I committed to finishing anything she had started. I asked Him to make her ceiling my floor. I promised to be faithful. Then I watched myself pick up the invisible mantle from her and place it on me as I sang about 20 verses of "I'll go where you want me to go, dear Lord. I'll do what you want me to do."

Mom died the next morning. At her funeral, my brother Phill showed a video he had made of her life, including interviews with her eight children. It ended with the recording of a song that best summed up her nearly 60 years of walking with Jesus. Once delivered in a clear, youthful voice, now in broken, crackly tones, we heard our mother sing, "I fell in love with the Nazarene."

Today, as I write this chapter about purpose, my mother continues to impact me in a couple of profound ways: First, her homegoing serves as a constant reminder that the clock is ticking in *my* life and that I must be diligent about numbering my days (see Ps. 90:12) and finishing the course I've been called to pursue. Second, I'm reminded of a dream she had of me receiving what she believed to be God's call on my life when I was a little girl. She dreamed she heard a knock at the front door and opened to a man who said, "I've come for Lynda." Mom looked over his shoulder and saw other children in the back of the station wagon he had driven. The man continued, "I won't take Lynda now, but I'll be back for her, as I have something for her to do."

I thought of Mom's dream this morning when I spent time with God. I asked Him, "How am I doing with accomplishing the work You sent me to do?" The knowledge of that calling on my life coupled with the shortness of the time to complete it filled me with urgency once again. So this chapter will come from a pretty deep place in my heart.

Most of us didn't get much encouragement or enlightenment concerning how to pursue our life purpose. So it's time to play catch-up both for ourselves and for our role as influencers of others, and vision plays a major part.

You Were Born on Purpose

One evening, I drove by an empty lot near our home, and a couple of things caught my eye—a bulldozer and a large picture mounted on a sign. It wasn't just any picture. It displayed a beautiful hotel complete with green shutters, which they clearly planned to build there. The idle bulldozer was parked in the middle of a large pile of dirt and was obviously poised to begin again where it had left off. Recently, friends of ours came to town and stayed in that now-completed, green-shuttered, exactly-like-the-sign-showed hotel. By keeping the end result constantly in mind, builders and bulldozer operators worked day after day until the hotel in the picture became a reality. They kept their eyes not on where they were but where they needed to go, and every building decision they made brought them closer to that goal.

Your purpose is much like that too. Before you were born, God drew up a big picture of your life and your assignment in it: "Your eyes saw my unformed substance, and in Your book all the days [of my life] were written before ever they took shape, when as yet there was none of them" (Ps. 139:16, *AMP*). I have heard this verse described as God writing a before-your-birth baby book about the beginning, middle and end of your life. It details every part of every day of every bit of your existence and assignment. Other than getting to know Him through the new birth, completing what He's called you to do is the most essential goal of your life. You, too, must keep your eyes not on where you are but on where you need to go to make each and every decision accordingly.

A New Testament verse affirms God's intricate plan for you laid out since the beginning of time:

> For we are God's [own] handiwork (His workmanship), recreated in Christ Jesus, [born anew] that we may do those good works which God predestined (planned beforehand) for us [taking paths which He prepared ahead of time], that we should walk in them [living the good life which He prearranged and made ready for us to live] (Eph. 2:10, *AMP*).

The word "handiwork" or "workmanship" is the Greek word *poiema*, which means "that which is manufactured." It's a product or design produced by an artisan. You are God's poem, His work of art! He truly *does* have plans for you. And the Holy Spirit Helper is with you to reveal every detail of your life's picture and to guide you in bringing it about.

In the last chapter, we talked about how you're gifted. Your *gift* is the talent you were born with. Your *purpose* is the mission you were created to accomplish. But your *vision* is like the sign at the hotel—the ability to see your gifting at work and your purpose accomplished before it ever happens. Vision displays God's purposes and plans for you, unrolls circumstances that don't yet exist, shows what is possible for your life, and peers into the eternal, invisible realm and brings them into now.

Do you know your gifts? Are you aware of your purpose in life? Have you been able to envision yourself fulfilling the purpose to which you've been assigned?

When my daughter Courtney was in fourth grade, I received a call from her teacher after they'd gone on a field trip. They had a Down's syndrome girl in their class named Sarah. Courtney has a personality that attracts lots of friends, and she's always the life of a party. But on their trip that day, Courtney kept checking on Sarah and including her with the rest of the girls. The teacher wanted me to know about my daughter's tender heart.

Twelve years later, Courtney went with her basketball team at the Christian college where she played to Costa Rica for a missions trip. When she returned, she told me how the rest of her team committed their lives to some type of missionary work, while she committed to helping hurt children. Today, Courtney is working as a counselor at Denver Children's hospital, helping very hurt children while she finishes her master's degree in counseling. Courtney, like you, has always been the *way* she is because of *why* she is. Courtney's assignment made *her;* she didn't make her assignment.

My daughter saw herself working with hurt children a long time ago. That vision helped her eliminate extraneous choices for subjects she studied and jobs she held through the years. If she hadn't been able to see herself doing this kind of work, she would probably be like many others—frustrated, clueless and unfocused about her life purpose. It would be like taking off in a car without a destination in mind and meandering as a result. There are lots of scenic roads, but you need to choose the ones that will deliver you to the place you need to go. The Bible talks about what happens to those who don't determine ahead of time where their purposed destination is taking them: "Where there is no vision, the people perish" (Prov. 29:18, *KJV*).

Other versions of that verse describe the results like this:

- "people cast off restraint" (*NIV*)
- "[the people] run wild" (*NLT*)
- "the people don't control themselves" (*NIRV*)
- "[the people] stumble all over themselves" (*THE MESSAGE*)
- "the people wander all over the place and never reach their assigned destination" (author's paraphrase)

Obviously, you not only need to know how you're gifted and what you're born to do, but you also need to be able to see the end result and your progress toward it. It happens by developing a relationship with the Holy Spirit, pressing into His wisdom and seeing your future as He sees it.

Fellow Purpose Finders

As you know, the Bible was penned to provide a lamp to your feet and a light to your pathway (see Ps. 119:105). It gives examples of many men and women who also owned places on the timeline of history and pieces of the purpose in God's great design. Let's look at a few of those portraits and how vision helped in the fulfillment of their individual callings.

Noah
Noah was born in the genealogy of Adam, 10 generations down the line. At birth, his father, Lamech, named his boy "Noah,"

and talked about his purpose (see Gen. 5:29). Little is told about that purpose coming to maturity until after Noah was 500 years old (he lived to be 950)—except that he had three sons. Meanwhile, God was aligning His own details while also preparing Noah for what was to come through his faithfulness in the smaller things.

As the world grew more wicked, Noah grew more in favor with God (see Gen. 6:8). Then the day came when he received his full job description. God told him the "what" and "how" of his assignment (see vv. 14-15). God also told Noah "why" (see vv. 17-18).

Noah heard God's instruction and obeyed (see v. 22). And he kept hearing and obeying for more than 120 years during the building of his ark. He believed it would rain even though it had never rained before. He believed he was chosen to save the remnant on the earth, even when bystanders held him in derision. Why? Because he had seen God's big picture for his life and heard His instructions. That's what he kept in the forefront of his mind and heart, and that's what sustained him.

Abraham

After the flood, God used Noah's three children to re-people the earth, one of whom was Shem. Nine generations into Shem's bloodline, a son was born whose name was Abram (later changed to Abraham). God spoke to his ears, telling him to leave his home because He wanted to make him a great and blessed nation (see Gen. 12:1-3) and to allow his descendants to inherit the new land of Canaan (see Gen. 12:7). Then, God spoke twice to Abraham about his eyes:

> *Lift your eyes now and look* from the place where you are . . . for all the land which you see I give to you and your descendants forever. And I will make your descendants as the dust of the earth; so that if a man could number the dust of the earth, then your descendants also could be numbered. Arise, walk in the land through its length and its width, for I give it to you (Gen. 13:14-17, emphasis added).

Then He [God] brought him [Abraham] outside and said, *"Look now toward heaven, and count the stars if you are able to number them."* And He said to him, "So shall your descendants be" (Gen. 15:5, emphasis added).

Though Abraham questioned how this could happen at his age (see Gen. 15:2-3), he tucked God's instructions in his heart and kept the vision before his eyes as he continued to fulfill his purpose.

Rahab

Rahab was a prostitute in Jericho going about her "business." Her story is told in Joshua 2. She'd heard how God had made the Israelites successful in their conquests, and she observed how the land was fainthearted because of them (see Josh. 2:9). So when Joshua's two spies arrived at her house, she did what lots of us women would do: she bartered her way into becoming part of the action. She would hide the spies from the king of Jericho in exchange for the salvation of her and her family.

The spies agreed and told her to tie a scarlet cord in her window, and their lives would be spared. No doubt Rahab kept her eyes on the scarlet-cord reminder of her crucial, grafted-in role during the turbulent days that followed in Jericho. The walls fell, but her part in God's plan continued, and He honored this gutsy woman's faith. The first chapter of Matthew lists the genealogy of Jesus through Joseph. Guess whose name appears in His bloodline? You guessed it. Rahab the prostitute (see Matt. 1:5). Then in the Hebrews 11 faith hall of fame, Scripture attributed Rahab's ability to envision her part in God's purpose to her willingness to believe (see Heb. 11:31).

Esther

Esther was a Jewish orphan who was raised by her cousin Mordecai. She learned from him that the Jews faced possible annihilation in the Persian Empire at the hand of the king's chancellor. Esther had been married to the king for five years and had kept her Jewish heritage a secret. But when Mordecai asked her to help

with the situation, she did—even at the risk of her own life. Mordecai had assured her that if she didn't intervene, someone else
would. Esther, however, heard the call and saw her place in God's
plan for preserving His chosen people. She saw her appointment
in history's lineup "for such a time as this" (Esther 4:14) and even
declared, "if I perish, I perish" (v. 16). Esther envisioned her purpose and set out to fulfill it, even if it cost her life. Her choice pre-
served the Jewish people.

Mary

What a calling Mary received! In Luke 1:26-38, God sent the angel
Gabriel to open Mary's eyes to her purpose. He let her know that
God favored her and that He was with her. Then He gave her a
glimpse of her future: "you will conceive," "you will bear a son,"
"you will call His name Jesus." Gabriel also turned her eyes to who
her Son would be: "He will be great," "He will be called the Son of
the Most High," "God will give Him the throne," "He will reign
over the house of Jacob forever" and "His kingdom will have no
end." What did Mary do with all these visions into what would be?
She set aside her doubts and pondered all these things she was seeing in her heart (see Luke 2:17-19). That's what kept her going
through all the incredible things that followed.

Phoebe

Only two verses in Scripture were given to Phoebe's life (see Rom.
16:1-2), but that's part of the beauty of her ministry. Without fan-
fare, these two verses, written by Paul, involve his recommenda-
tion of Phoebe as he encouraged the Romans to accept her. Why?
Turns out she was a single woman, who became Paul's spokesperson in Rome for two years before he arrived. Paul wrote the book
of Romans, and she delivered it to the Gentiles. It was Paul's most
complete declaration of the gospel. Phoebe didn't find reasons for
needing to attend to the responsibilities of her single life. Instead,
she set her schedule aside and envisioned her important role in ex-
panding the gospel to include Gentiles for all time. She got busy
on the present because she saw her important role in the future.

What About *Your* Purpose?

The ways in which these Bible characters used vision to fulfill *their* purpose tell you much about how to fulfill *yours*. One thing you must keep in mind, however: Those in the Old Testament didn't have the Holy Spirit, while those in the New Testament did, and so do you. He assigns it, reveals it, and helps accomplish it. All you need to do is follow His lead while keeping these seven truths in mind:

1. Clarity

Not many people download God's complete plan for them in one sitting as Noah did. When I read in the New Testament about Noah's great faith (see Heb. 11:7), I don't find myself envying him for his notable trust in God. Instead, I feel a little jealous about how completely and immediately God let him know his assignment on earth.

The Holy Spirit hasn't done the same with me thus far, and He probably hasn't done the same for you. Instead, He usually provides instruction in increments—words here, visions there—as He did for Abraham. What we *do* know is that He *does* do it (see Isa. 30:21).

Keep track of what you *know* God has told you regarding what you've been called to do. Then as the Holy Spirit adds new details, document those as well. And remember to envision it! It's okay that some details are still missing. As you continue this process, slowly you will find your purpose picture becoming clearer. Find it out, and then walk it out.

2. Favor

Doors open when they shouldn't. Someone listens to you when they shouldn't. You get opportunities when you shouldn't. Provision comes when it shouldn't.

These events are evidence of the favor of God on your life because you have accepted your assignment. Esther feared that she would die, but instead she received God's favor for herself and God's people. He brought favor on Phoebe so the Gentiles would receive the gospel.

The Holy Spirit goes before you to clear the way, provide the means and cause others to unknowingly cooperate with you in fulfilling that assignment. The Holy Spirit wraps favor around what you've been called to do:

> For You are the glory of their strength, and in Your favor our horn is exalted. For our shield belongs to the Lord, and our king to the Holy One of Israel (Ps. 89:17-18).

> For they did not gain possession of the land by their own sword nor did their own arm save them; but it was Your right hand, Your arm, and the light of Your countenance, because You favored them (Ps. 44:3).

You accept the assignment and then leave the details to the Holy Spirit.

3. Timing

Noah may have had the big picture of his purpose, but God took His time about bringing it to pass. God declares the end from the beginning (see Isa. 46:10). Then little by little He shows those things to you (see Jer. 33:3)—things you can take to the bank, no matter how long it is delayed.

In Habakkuk 2:1-3, the prophet shows how you do that. First, "watch to see what He will say to me, and what I will answer when I am corrected" (v. 1). Give the Holy Spirit consistent opportunities to talk to you as you keep your spiritual eyes and ears open. It's a good time to journal your prayers, and watch to see what God says to you.

Second, "Write the vision and make it plain on tablets, that he may run who reads it" (v. 2). Keep track of the clues the Holy Spirit has already provided and look at them often with your spiritual eyes.

Third, accept the process. "For the vision is yet for an appointed time; but at the end it will speak, and it will not lie. Though it tarries, wait for it; because it will surely come, it will not tarry" (v. 3). It may take more time than you'd like, but it *will* happen (see Gen. 21:2).

4. Focus

Your assignment is geographical. You don't belong *anywhere*; you belong *somewhere*. But your calling is also not done in isolation. It's an important part, but only a part of the ministry of the Kingdom neighborhood as a whole. Each person builds on what the others did before him (see 1 Cor. 3:10), and it's important for the collective Body that you do your part well. Realizing this truth will send you a big step forward in your maturity and toward fulfilling your assignment.

5. Preparation

In many cases, God delays in order to properly prepare His people for their work. He teaches and perfects us. As we submit to *being* taught and perfected, we are, in fact, fulfilling a portion of our assignment. The visions of these Bible examples sustained them through their preparation time. Every day took them (and it takes you and me) toward the completion of the final goal. Your preparation is part of that process, so surrender yourself joyfully to it.

6. Qualifications

After receiving his call, Moses argued with God that he couldn't talk plainly. Abraham said he was too old, while Jeremiah said he was too young. Sarai laughed, Esther feared for her life, and Mary wondered how it could be so. You and I will never figure out why the Holy Spirit chooses whom He does. But we see that He always chooses and uses those whose hearts belong totally to Him. Continue to move with the Holy Spirit as He guides you, and continue to get to know and love Him in the journey.

7. Method of Operation

All these Bible examples realized that the moment they received their calling, its fulfillment was underway, so they kept their eyes and ears open to subsequent instructions. I call it "proceeding from the knowns." My mother called it "getting your M.O." (your method of operation). Sometimes I just write down what I *do* know to do and move on from there. The Holy Spirit wants us to know His will more than we want to know it.

I often turn Proverbs 16:3 into a prayer about my purpose: "Commit your works to the LORD, and your thoughts will be established." The verse becomes most relevant when we look at the meaning of the words:

- To "commit" means "to roll down or away; to remove; to roll our works into God's care." It's the picture of a camel burdened with a heavy load. To remove the load, the camel kneels down, tilts far to one side and the load rolls off.

- "Works" means "transactions, activities, products, properties, businesses, deeds, labors, things made, occupations or things offered."

- "Established" means "to be erect, stand perpendicular, set up, establish, fix, appoint, render sure, certain, confirm, fasten, firm, be fitted, be fixed, frame, ordain, order, perfect, make provision, make ready, set aright, be stable, stablish, stand."

The Holy Spirit is the Assigner of the assignment, and you and I are the carriers of it. We accept that assignment, stay close to the Assigner and don't worry about how it will come to fruition. All He wants from us is our growing love and faith in Him. Then He puts the pieces together in the right way at the right time, and the mission is accomplished.

A Twofold Process

God could have spoken anything and everything into existence whenever and wherever He wanted. Instead, He chose to use the people He created and loved to accomplish His work and fulfill

His desires. The establishment of His kingdom on earth is like a factory moving here from a foreign country. The management brings with it the business and their ways of doing things, but they hire local workers to do the work, to manufacture the products conceived in the mind of the owner.

That's the way God designed for His Kingdom to be brought about on earth as it is in heaven. Our part is twofold: first to know Him, and second to fulfill our individual assignments in His Kingdom work.

Whether you have realized it or not, the Holy Spirit has been guiding you your whole life toward fulfillment of the assignment you received when you were little. As you allow all the separate aspects of your life to converge and head together toward the same, predetermined end, everything you will ever need to fulfill your life's calling becomes possible through the Holy Spirit. In the process, you can change your life from status quo and "also lived" to awesome, exciting and fulfilling.

I received a birthday card once that said, "When you were born, the angels in heaven announced, 'Look out below!' " Don't look through a straw at your life. Climb out of your box. Dream big. Move along with the Holy Spirit. Your best days are ahead. You ain't seen nothin' yet. That's the message to you from the Holy Spirit today. *"Trust Me. Come along with Me. I've got big plans for you."*

> Do not remember the former things, nor consider the things of old. Behold, I will do a new thing, now it shall spring forth; shall you not know it? I will even make a road in the wilderness and rivers in the desert (Isa. 43:18-19).

> I will instruct you and teach you in the way you should go; I will guide you with My eye (Ps. 32:8).

So keep on keeping on. Keep on following where the Holy Spirit is leading you. Keep on fulfilling your purpose.

*M*ake It Yours
Live Out Your Purpose

Your Beginning . . .
Look up Isaiah 46:10, read it out loud, and then summarize its meaning below.

_____
_____
_____
_____

Look up Romans 9:10-12 and Jeremiah 1:5, and then read these verses out loud. What role did God play in both the birth and the purpose of Jacob and Jeremiah?

_____
_____
_____
_____

Now substitute your information for Jacob's and Jeremiah's in these two passages:

> When _____ [insert your mother's name] also had conceived by one man, _____ [insert your father's name], (for the children not yet being born, nor having done any good or evil, that the purpose of God according to election might stand, not of works but of Him who calls), it was said to her, "_____ _____" [if applicable, insert one or two alerts your mother might have received regarding your calling] (Rom. 9:10-12).

> Before I formed _____ [insert your name] in the womb I knew you; before _____ [was] born I sanctified you; I ordained you _____

[insert what you know so far that He ordained you to be]
(Jer. 1:5).

Was your birth an accident? Why or why not?

_____

_____

_____

_____

Is your purpose and calling undecided? Why or why not?

_____

_____

_____

_____

Your Middle . . .
PERT (Program Evaluation Review Technique), a naval term created in the 1950s, describes a technique that is used today to accomplish various projects, such as building an addition onto a
business. PERT involves a starting point, an ending point, the necessary steps in between and the times required to accomplish each
step. Our lives, in fact, reflect a sort of PERT. We're born, we die,
and in-between stuff happens that often doesn't make sense. But
in the end, we see how God makes good out of the bad (see Gen.
50:20) and even uses the bad to help us fulfill our purpose.

Read Genesis 37 and 39–47. Joseph's story began when he envisioned his calling (see 37:5). But as he went forward with that calling, unfair things happened to him. Here's the PERT that emerged
from Joseph's life:

X	X	X	X	X	X	X
Home	Hole	Slavery	Betrayal	Prison	Release	Reward

We don't know how much time elapsed between each event,
but we *do* know that the total time comprised about 16 years. Yet

even while Joseph was going through hard things, he continued to remain close to God and embrace his assignment. God brought him favor as a result (see Gen. 39:4,21). In the end, God redeemed Joseph, made him second in command in Egypt, and delivered the Israelites through him. Read Genesis 37:28. How did God get him to the right place at the right time?

_____

_____

_____

_____

God made even the bad stuff become a part of the fulfillment of Joseph's assignment. In hindsight, it's easy to see the reason for everything that happened in Joseph's life. Ask Joseph, however, at any time during the process and he would not have been so confident. But he *did* have his dream—the vision of his calling—to hold on to.

Create your own PERT. Insert all the major events—good and bad—that have happened in your life. Include the time element for each event.

X   X   X   X   X   X   X
_____

Now draw a frame around your PERT and view it as a picture of your life. Based on Joseph's example, what truths can you list regarding everything that lies ahead for you?

_____

_____

_____

_____

Your End . . .
In Ecclesiastes 1:3, we read, "What profit has a man from all his labor?" (Eccles. 1:3). The word for "profit" in this verse is the He-

brew word *yitron*. It means "gain" and refers to the fixed, unchanging values in life. *Yitron* is the part that lasts. *Yitron* is the aspect of you that will keep living long after you're gone. Remember the old saying, "Only one life, 'twill soon be passed. Only what's done for Christ will last"? *Yitron* is what's done for Christ (your fulfilled assignment), what you will someday lay down at His feet, and what will determine your rewards. Describe the connection of *yitron* to your assignment.

_____

_____

_____

_____

How can you use *yitron* to help you number your days (see Ps. 90:12) from this point forward?

_____

_____

_____

_____

Compose your own prayer confession below about your commitment to fulfilling your purpose. Use some of the verses and truths we discussed in this chapter. Be specific, be bold, and be thankful for the work He's called you to do.

PRAYER CONFESSION

Holy Spirit,

_____

_____

_____

_____

_____

Amen.

𝒯rust but Verify

He [the Holy Spirit] will glorify Me [Jesus], for He will take of what is Mine and declare it to you.

JOHN 16:14

Missouri boasts of being the "Show Me" state. It's okay that it borrows that distinction, but if you ask me, the title belongs to us women. We're the ones in the real "show me" state—of mind, that is. We like to read and be told, but most of all, we like to *see*. The proof is in the pudding. We like for our husbands to put their money where their mouth is. We like promises, but we like revelations even more.

I had a neighbor once who apparently enjoyed the personal way with which I approached my faith. I often counseled and studied the Bible with her regarding several challenges she faced in her marriage and in other areas of her life.

One day, she came to my front door excited about an "experience" she had had. Weary from praying for an answer to a huge problem, she described looking out the window at the snow. Nothing was visible anywhere but white. Cars and roads and bushes were covered. But suddenly she saw a small light beside a neighbor's sidewalk peeking out from beneath the white blanket. She took it as a sign. Her light was shining through. Her answer had arrived. Her future looked bright.

Excitedly, she told me all this from my front porch, even before she came inside. I ushered her in and directed her to my couch. I was happy with the joy that I saw on her face as recently I had seen only tears. I didn't want to dampen her exuberance, but I also didn't want her to be misguided.

So I pulled out my Bible. "That's wonderful," I said. "The Holy Spirit could, indeed, be talking to you, encouraging you today. But what do we know for sure? What does the Bible say about God hearing your prayers? What does the Word tell us about His answers?"

And so we went to Scripture. We looked up different verses that dealt with her circumstances. By the time she walked back out my door, I hadn't taken *away* from her experience. Instead, I had added to that event verses that assured her she was on the right track. However, now she had based her confidence on the eternal Word of God, and doing so would keep her from placing her trust in less reliable things.

The Personal Touch

Some critics have faulted the charismatic movement as being too experiential. They say that too much theology rises from things seen or heard or felt rather than from the Bible. They maintain that experiences are not a valid source of truth.

I agree. If anyone at any time bases any truth on anything other than the Word of God, he or she is in error.

Having said that, I'm a woman, *and* some of my ancestry comes from Missouri. And so . . . I like to be *shown* too. It was the visible, tangible, measurable evidence of my mother's faith that caused me to want what she had. While my dad loved God and served as a mentor and spiritual giant for most of his life, I loved that God spoke clearly to my mom. I was intrigued that she heard from Him. I wanted to also be able to see things He revealed.

What I didn't want to do is base my faith upon experience alone, and neither should you. It's okay to see the light under the snow and apply what we believe to be the interpretation. But we should always go straight to Scripture for truths that we don't have to guess at or try to interpret. Then we can use our supernatural experiences to confirm that truth and make it more personal.

The whole process reminds me of an old phrase, "trust but verify," made popular by the late Ronald Reagan. When Reagan spoke these words, he was often discussing relations with the Soviet Union, and he almost always presented it as a translation of the Russian proverb *doveryai, no proveryai*—trust, but verify. At the signing of the INF Treaty, he used it once again, and his counterpart Mikhail Gorbachev responded: "You repeat that at every meeting," to which Reagan answered, "I like it."

I like it, too, and have adapted the phrase to apply to personal encounters—trust [experiences], but verify. A specific procedure has been set up for us to receive divine information and instruction. The Holy Spirit hears from Jesus, and He passes on that same message to us.

He [the Holy Spirit] will glorify Me [Jesus], for He will take of what is Mine and declare it to you (John 16:14).

We have inside information. The One living inside us is a member of and is privy to everything going on in the mind of God the Father and Jesus the Son. Then when we ask, He shares that inside track with us. And yes, He does so in a variety of ways. You have read how often the Holy Spirit speaks to me in dreams. He also instructs me through other people, shows me images and speaks unfamiliar words that provide instruction once I discover their meanings.

Before I moved to Colorado to work for Focus on the Family, I was making my way through the bank drive-thru to pay my mortgage. As I waited, I heard the words "purveyor of instruments." As I pulled away from the bank and again while I was driving home on Cox Road, I heard the phrase repeated, "purveyor of instruments." I didn't know the meaning of the word "purveyor." The dictionary told me it was "a person who brings edibles to a large number of people, and in England, it's a person who brings food to the king's household."

So what was I to do with this information that I felt might be helping me define the mission of my life? I had just finished my doctorate, had not yet begun writing or speaking and was totally unsure about what to do next. I could discount my bank drive-thru experience as something I imagined, or I could run out and base my whole life's ministry and calling on it. Many do. I chose a third option, however. I acknowledged what I had heard and put it on a shelf until I understood it better. Then I moved forward, keeping it in the back of my mind as I prayed, studied, sought God's direction and waited for Him to open the right doors for me. As I look back, I believe the Holy Spirit was describing for me my role and assignment in feeding God's people spiritual food through spoken and written words.

Jesus said that His sheep hear His voice (see John 10:27). In addition to getting to know Him, He wants you to learn to recognize and obey when He speaks. You and I are His sheep, and His voice comes in the Person of the Holy Spirit. It's one of His main jobs, like interpreters at the UN, who take the words of a speaker and turn them into languages that each hearer can understand. In the end, every member of the audience, regardless of the language they speak, comprehends the message.

Our interpreter is the Holy Spirit. God gave us the *Logos* Word of God, but He also provided for the *Rhema* Word of God through the Holy Spirit. The *Logos* is the *stated* or *written* Word of God. It's the Bible. The *Rhema,* on the other hand, is the *revealed* Word of God. *Rhema* is the Holy Spirit talking, the Spirit of revelation. If you can't hear Him, you won't have the *Rhema* for this time and for your situations. *Rhema* is your source of direction from God, and it never contradicts *Logos.* Being able to trust in *Rhema* while verifying it with the *Logos* is foundational to an effective Christian experience.

Rhema communicates knowledge:

> Now we have received, not the spirit of the world, but the Spirit who is from God, that we might know the things that have been freely given to us by God (1 Cor. 2:12).

> But you have an anointing from the Holy One, and you know all things (1 John 2:20).

> But the anointing which you have received from Him abides in you, and you do not need that anyone teach you; but as

the same anointing teaches you concerning all things, and is true, and is not a lie, and just as it has taught you, you will abide in Him (1 John 2:27).

Rhema shows you right choices:

Your ears shall hear a word behind you, saying, "This is the way, walk in it" (Isa. 30:21).

Rhema also reveals the future:

Call to Me, and I will answer you, and show you great and mighty things, which you do not know (Jer. 33:3).

As the Holy Spirit takes what belongs in the mind of Jesus and shares this *Rhema* with you, He not only personalizes it, but He also does so creatively. He might speak Jesus' mind one time through your child's words and the next time through something you see in nature. It's not that He's adding on to what has already been spoken through the *Logos* of Scripture. Instead, He reminds and reinforces and brings alive something that's already there by providing the *Rhema*. And He expects us to verify these *Rhema* experiences He gives us by going to *Logos*. To "verify" means "to prove to be true or correct; to establish the truth of; to confirm; to substantiate; to confirm or establish the authenticity of by examination or competent evidence; to authenticate."

Even in Scripture, the biggest examples of verification began with personal experience (*Rhema*) as God made His Word (*Logos*) come alive in a real way for particular individuals. Before Jesus ascended, this happened as God's Spirit spoke through His Son. Let's see some examples of how this came about.

Seeing Is Believing

Jesus saw a man who was blind from birth. The disciples saw him too. They wanted to know what or whom had caused the blindness. Had his parents done something wrong? I find it even more laughable that the disciples wanted to know if the man had committed some sin that had caused this horrible affliction to plague him. Hello! He'd been blind from birth. He would have had to have sinned in the womb or in another life, so I think they could safely mark that one off as a rhetorical question. They asked it nonetheless, but Jesus did not give a rhetorical answer: "Neither this man nor his parents sinned, but that the works of God should be revealed in him" (John 9:3).

Now, the works or *ergon* of God had been revealed since the beginning of time. Throughout the Old Testament, God did things to and for individuals to confirm His works. In Exodus chapters 7–11, God sent 10 plagues to Egypt and 10 ways to deliver His people from these plagues while others around them perished—just to show His works and to prove who He was. He'd already told Moses in Exodus 3 that He was "I AM." But then He went on to prove His works when the God I AM rolled back the Red Sea and sent manna for them to eat.

And He was still showing these works in John 9. In a most unconventional way, Jesus spit on the ground, picked up the muddy mixture and rubbed it on the eyes of the blind man (see v. 6). Talk about holy ground! Just as saliva from the Savior of the world made contact with regular ol' dirt, the works of God straight out of heaven made contact with an ordinary man. Jesus told him to go and wash in the pool of Siloam. The man did so. Then he returned to Jesus, his blindness healed. He was able to see for the first time in his life.

Cynics descended on him. Neighbors and Pharisees looked critically on God's works that had been revealed in the man. They asked, "How were your eyes opened?" And the formerly blind man told them what had happened. So the Jews called on the parents to verify the facts, and they did. Yes, this was their son, and yes, he'd been healed. Then they told the critics to go ask the son himself (see v. 23).

That's when the best part of the story occurred. The healed son said he didn't know the answers to all their questions. But one thing he did know: "I was blind, now I see" (John 9:25).

Every time I read those words, I get a lump in my throat. I can't explain the many times the Holy Spirit has given me instruction, but He has. I don't understand why He takes the time to speak to me about even trivial issues, but He does. Certain verses in my Bible are soiled from my dragging my finger across promises for people or circumstances that I'm still trusting Him for. And I can do this because of what I've already seen Him do.

That's also why this man's answer was so simple. "I don't know the answers to your questions, guys. I just know I was blind and now I see." Jesus had individualized Himself to this man in need. The naysayers kept trying to get him to change his story, but he kept telling what Jesus had done. This would never do, so they cast him out. They got rid of him. They shut him up.

But Jesus found him and identified Himself as the Son of God. By doing so, He verified the experience the man had had: "You have both seen Him and it is He who is talking with you" (John 9:37). And the man became a follower of Jesus!

The Jewish law and the Scriptures were well known in those days, so the man had probably heard it some time in his life. But then he had an experience. God made it personal. God brought the words off the parchment pages into the everyday life of a person, making the word real and irrefutable. Why? So that the works of God could be revealed in this specific man.

Jesus went on to justify the reason He did what He did and the way He did it: "For judgment I have come into this world, that those who do not see may see, and that those who see may be made blind" (John 9:39). The man who was blind had his eyes opened. The Pharisees whose eyes had studied the Scriptures were blind to what He had accomplished. The man was blind to the reality of the truth until the experience, then he believed and went on to discover more. The Pharisees who explained away everything rejected the experience and relegated God to words only.

Let's look at another experience of where Jesus intersected the Logos with real-life experience.

Encounter at the Well

Jesus had made an amazing impact on the world. Again, an unnamed woman in Samaria must have heard about these remarkable feats that had happened to other people. Even before emails, faxes, phones and texting, news spread fast—especially good news.

One day the woman went to the well to draw water just as she'd done the day before. But this day was different. She arrived at the well to find a Stranger sitting beside the well, resting from His journey. The Stranger asked the woman for a drink of water. The woman questioned why He (a Jew) was even talking to her (a half-breed Samaritan). After all, Jews usually had no dealings with Samaritans. What she didn't know is that not only was He talking to her, but also He'd changed His travel plans from Judea to Galilee so that He could go through Samaria (see John 4:1-4).

Jesus quickly cut to the reason for His visit. He described the difference between the water she'd come to draw and the living water she'd come to need. He offered that which would cause her to never thirst again. Many knew well the words of Isaiah: "Therefore with joy you will draw water from the wells of salvation" (Isa. 12:3). But here was Jesus, who'd gone out of His way to personally deliver the truth of those words through experience.

He proved that He knew her intimately. Though they'd just met, He described information that only she knew, then He went on to tell her about the pathway to salvation, and the Holy Spirit was the integral part of that pathway:

> You worship what you do not know; we know what we worship, for salvation is of the Jews. But the hour is coming, and now is, when the true worshipers will worship the Father in spirit and truth; for the Father is seeking such to worship Him. God is Spirit, and those who worship Him must worship in spirit and truth (John 4:22-24).

Alive with new birth; aglow with the Holy Spirit's enablement. The woman wanted what Jesus described. By the time the disciples returned and questioned why Jesus was engaged in conversation with a woman—and a Samaritan woman at that—she had left her watering pot behind and headed out to tell others about Jesus. And people came to Him because of her:

And many of the Samaritans of that city believed in Him because of the word of the woman who testified, "He told me all that I ever did." . . . And many more believed because of His own word. Then they said to the woman, "Now we believe, not because of what you said, for we ourselves have heard Him and we know that this is indeed the Christ, the Savior of the world" (John 4:39,41-42).

Like the blind man healed in John 9, Jesus accomplished far bigger things than the issues at hand. The Holy Spirit doesn't force His personal experiences and visitations on those who fail to hear, see or believe what He has to impart. But when He finds that person who does, He uses that willing person to accomplish far greater things for the Kingdom. I want to be one of those people, don't you?

I Was There

Neither this man nor this woman could ever have anyone talk them out of the truth that Jesus brought. After all, they were there when He met them personally. They were there when He proved He knew them. They were there when they realized they were deeply and eternally loved and known.

Verses in my Bible are outlined and highlighted and contain notes beside them. I have hundreds of notes on Scriptures I have studied. But buried most deeply in my heart are the personal experiences I have had. My faith can be robbed of some of the promises in the Word when I'm faced with prolonged troubles, but nothing can ever take away my intimate encounters with God. I was there. I have the dates written beside some of the verses He personally spoke to me. I have words reminding me of lessons He took the time to teach me.

So how do we keep this in balance? How do we not overdo the Rhema experiences and under-do the Logos Word?

When I was conducting research for my doctorate, I learned to "triangulate" my data. As I observed evidence of something in one setting, I began to search for it in another. If the evidence failed to repeat itself at a different time, I concluded that it was not valid and was an outlier, an anomaly, instead.

Your standard is the Word of God. Begin and end by knowing Scriptures connected to your situation; but in between, enjoy experience. Have confidence in the dreams He gives you. Open your ears to wise instructional confirmation He sends along your path. As the sheep, your job is to hear and trust, and His is to do the speaking. Don't relegate Him to speaking only through His Word. Allow Elohim, who created the flowers and sky and moon and stars, to creatively talk to you today through His Spirit. Never steer away from Scripture, but always be open to other wonderful, personal ways He will speak to you. If you do, you're in for an exciting adventure. And when you do, the Holy Spirit will become more real and personally yours than He ever has been before.

Choosing the Good Part

I sat with my pen poised before me, taking notes in the class I was taking at Fuller Theological Seminary on the Gospels. That particular night, the professor taught from Luke 10 about Mary and Martha. You know the story: Mary sat at Jesus' feet while Martha worked in the kitchen.

Suddenly, I flashed back to the summer of 1986, the beginning of my journey as a single mom. My newborn son was sleeping in his car seat, and my two- and four-year-old daughters were playing in the puddles on the driveway while I washed our family van. I had surrendered my life to Christ the previous fall and had pored over every verse and radio and television teaching I could find for a crash course in spiritual growth. As I stood with the sudsy sponge in my hand, I prayed, "God, I don't thank You for what I'm going through, but I do thank You that I now have time to spend with You."

Immediately, I heard the words spoken to my heart, "You've chosen the good part."

What? Where? Who? Confused, I finished washing the van, but later that afternoon, I heard the words again: "You've chosen the good part."

Once more, I pushed it aside when no explanations were forthcoming.

That night, I put the kids to bed and read my Bible before going to sleep myself. As I reached to turn off my green ginger-jar lamp, I heard the words a third time: "You've chosen the good part."

I turned the light back on and prayed, "God, I don't know where these words come from." Then I heard Him say, "Martha and Mary."

I pulled my Bible back from the nightstand and looked up the passage. I found it in Luke 10. When Martha criticized Mary for not helping her with the chores, Jesus affirmed Mary for her total devotion to Him. "Mary has chosen that good part, which will not be taken away from her" (Luke 10:42).

That night in my theology class, some 15 years later, the professor taught us the academic meanings of those words, but I found myself lost in the personal part I had experienced so many years before. I looked up at the ceiling and smiled at the God who had taken the time to bring His eternal Word into real time—my time. The Truth had broken into my life circumstances in an experiential way. Heaven invaded earth on behalf of a single mom who dared to look to God for her way forward.

What happened to me in 1986 didn't take away from what I was learning in 2001. My actual *Rhema* experience did not replace the *Logos* words of Scripture. Instead, like the healed blind man and the touched Samaritan woman, this personal experience made me want more. It brought the words alive to me. It personalized the promises as ones I will not forget. I will also never allow anyone to talk me out of what I was there to witness.

No, experience alone should not create the foundation for your beliefs. But just try it. Try opening your heart and eyes and tuning in your ears for any experience the Holy Spirit chooses to throw in just because He loves you.

Trust [experience], but always verify. Trust the *Rhema* experiences He gives you, but always verify them with the *Logos* of Scripture. What a way to live life! What a way to make His love for you come alive.

Make It Yours
Keep Your Experiences Solid

Write out a brief history of your encounters (or lack of them) with the *Rhema* experiences of the Holy Spirit.

_____

_____

_____

_____

_____

When it comes to the experiential part of your faith, you should trust, but verify; verify, but trust. Both are important. Remember this verse we discussed?

> For judgment I have come into this world, that those who do not see may see, and that those who see may be made blind (John 9:39).

The Pharisees were heavy on verifying but light on trusting. As a result, they missed out on anything experiential the Holy Spirit had to provide. The man learned to trust after he was healed, but he learned to verify after he met up with Jesus in the end and surrendered his life to Him. The Body of Christ is full of those who trust and also with those who verify. Heaven will contain some of each. But the Holy Spirit is searching for those who will go all the way—those who will both trust and verify so that He can reveal Himself more fully to them. He's looking for those who believe with all their hearts that the same One who was present at creation and raised Jesus from the dead is inside of you and is available to speak in creative Rhema ways to you today. Every day of your life, you must decide:

• Are you only going to verify and relegate His messages just to what the Bible says?

• Are you only going to trust the additional experiences you believe you receive from Him and risk getting in error or going off the deep end?

• Or are you going to open yourself up and trust the variety of creative, promised *Rhema* communications from the Holy Spirit and then go to the Word for verification?

Explain what you will do and why.

_____

_____

_____

_____

_____

One of the ways you can maintain an ongoing dialogue with the Holy Spirit is by keeping a journal. I know—you've heard whole sermons at women's retreats about the importance of journals. Then, with all the best intentions, you started one, but it fizzled out. You never quite connected with that mode of communicating with giving and receiving in prayer. I know because that's the way I did it again and again and again. But one day, I couldn't help but catch the bug from someone who totally loved this method of two-way communication with the Trinity. I took my example from her; and now I would like to pass it on to you.

To begin, select an inexpensive, hardback journal. I go to Walmart to find these and don't use spiral ring notebooks, as they're not effective in filing and making later reference to. Date your first page and write on it any verses, quotes or sermon nuggets especially meaningful to you today.

Begin your dialogue: "Dear God" or "Wonderful Lord" or "Sweet Holy Spirit," then write out your thank-yous and praises until you say all that is on your heart. Title a next section "My Daughter," then keep your pen to the paper. Write what you feel flowing out of your spirit. Don't doubt. Don't second-guess. At worst, you'll write some glorious words on your own; but at best, you'll hear directly from the heart of Jesus through the Holy Spirit. The more you do it, the more you'll get comfortable with it and build confidence in its validity.

You may want to stop here some days, or you may want to move on to talking about specific needs in your life or in the life of others. Be open. Be bold (see Heb. 4:16). Once again, wait quietly and expectantly and allow Him to talk back to you. "My daughter . . ." End your time together with more written or spoken or sung praises and thank-yous.

If you try this process, you'll get comfortable with it and discover new ways of making it more your own. Most of all, you can forever settle the issue of whether or not God really still talks to His people.

Remember from this point forward that God's *Rhema* already belongs to you because of who you have living inside you. Memorize the following verse and the privileges that come to you because of it:

In all your ways acknowledge Him, and He shall direct your paths (Prov. 3:6).

"Ways" means "road, course, mode of action." It suggests specific opportunities you may encounter on a recurring basis. "Acknowledge" means "know by observation, investigation, reflection or firsthand experience." It means intimate contact. "Direct" means "to be straight, right, upright, pleasing, good." It means to make straight and right. Based on these word definitions, paraphrase this verse in your own words about what God's *Rhema* does for you daily.

_____

_____

_____

_____

_____

_____

PRAYER CONFESSION

Holy Spirit, wow! Thank You that You are as old and present as time itself but as new and fresh and available and relevant as my issues are today. Thank You that You take everything that is in the heart of Jesus and give it to me. Thank You for the Logos *I have come to love and rely on and use to confirm and order my steps. But thank You also for the* Rhema *that brings the* Logos *alive in real circumstances. Make me hear everything You have to say to me at any time. Lead me into greater depths in this area. You are glorious and good. I love You. Amen.*

12

$\mathscr{M}$aking the Holy Spirit at Home in *Your* Heart

Jesus answered and said to him, "If anyone loves Me, he will keep My word; and My Father will love him, and We will come to him and make Our home with him."
JOHN 14:23

I was in my mid-teens when I sat beside my dad in church that Sunday morning. We were visiting my uncle in southern Arizona. Everything about the church service that day seemed largely unremarkable, except for an old hymn they sang. It was called "Learning to Lean." I'd never heard it before, but its message—especially the chorus—quickly became a central theme for me:

> I'm learning to lean, learning to lean,
> Learning to lean on Jesus.
> Finding more power than I'd ever dreamed,
> I'm learning to lean on Jesus.[1]

As I listened to the song and read its words from the hymnal, I glanced at my dad, his head bowed in reverence to His Lord. He had devoted his life to what he believed, and *my* life stretched out before me. I could discard what he and Mom had given me and go another route or ride their coattails and keep things the same or take what I'd learned and build on it. What was *not* an option was to continue forever relying on them for help in troubled times, for prayer when I needed for God to come through. I continued to listen to the words of the song that morning and in the months and years to come, as I sang it at my piano; and the choices continued to spread out before me. The choices were mine to make.

Joshua raised his 700,000 "kids" to follow God's ways, but ultimately the choice came down to each individual person (see Josh. 24:15). Elijah admonished the people to no longer "falter between two opinions" (1 Kings 18:21). Today, I have a simple question for you: After learning what the Holy Spirit *can* be, how much do you actually see Him becoming in your life? I'm not talking about your salvation and the fact that He took up residence in you when you were born again. I'm talking about making Him at home there and welcoming everything He has to give. It's the difference between someone coming to stay with you and someone moving in with all her belongings.

In previous chapters, you looked at the Holy Spirit's story since before the world began and up to this moment in your life. You learned how He makes His entrance twice—when you are born again and when you are filled with Him. You discovered how He provides a language for you that keeps you connected to your homeland—heaven—and the wisdom available to you from there. You've realized that no matter what your need, that's His specialty and He loves helping you do life. You grasped the fact that because of Him, you get unlimited power to make the miraculous a normal way of existence. You comprehended the truth that when He moves into your life, He passes on His character, which He calls fruits, so that qualities such as peace and patience are already yours. You've taken another look at which gifts He has given you to accomplish your work for the kingdom. And you've seen His role in helping you fulfill your life purpose.

How much of this is actually taking place in your life? Are you happy where you are? Are there additional areas of your heart that you need to open up to Him?

For years, I leaned on my mom and dad, who leaned on God. The one you have leaned on may be your parent or pastor or friend or someone else. It kind of reminds me of watching someone learn to roller skate. As long as that person grabs hold of this person or that wall, he or she is never able to steady themselves—much less skate. Those who are truly serious about learning to do it for themselves, however, say, "Thanks, but no more!" and then head off on their own. Sure they fall and get banged up. But the results far outweigh the price they pay, and over time, they're able to skate anyplace at any time, even with no one else around.

Not long after I heard that song for the first time with my dad, my 16-year-old sister, Connie, and I took a vacation to a summer Bible camp with a 33-year-old friend of ours named Evelyn, and her 10-year-old daughter. I was 18; and to help pay for our trip, the three of us got a job at the Bible school checking attendees into a large annex that served as sleeping quarters for the event.

One night, I arrived to relieve Evelyn and assume my midnight-to-8 A.M. shift. As I approached the door of the annex, I saw Evelyn sitting beneath a tree close by. She was a severe diabetic, requiring 110 units of insulin three times each day. She'd told us what to do if she ever went into insulin shock. One look at her told me that's what was happening.

I ran back to our dormitory, woke up Connie, sent her to cover my work shift and got the dorm "mother" to assist me with bringing Evelyn to our room. Next, I ran to the hospital infirmary to get medical help. A nurse ran with me, her supplies in hand. We arrived at our room to an almost unconscious Evelyn. The nurse worked with Evelyn till she settled down, then left along with the dorm attendant. I assumed the crisis was over; but soon, Evelyn became delirious again. I fetched the dorm mother and nurse just like before. They stayed until Evelyn went back to sleep.

At about 5:00 A.M., with orange barely starting to color the dark sky, the crisis started all over again. I headed toward the door, but this time I stopped. I turned on the light and walked to the bottom right bunk bed where Evelyn lay. I knelt down, and I remember the prayer I prayed over her incoherent rant: "God, if

Mom and Dad were here, they'd know what to do and how to reach You, but they're not. There are lots of godly men and women here at this camp who know how to get hold of You, but they're not here either. It's just me, and I need help. Please heal Evelyn, in the name of Jesus Christ."

I turned out the light, not because things looked any better, but because I knew I had done all I could do. I climbed into the upper bunk of the left bed, faced the wall and gave in to my exhaustion. I don't know how long I was asleep, but suddenly I was awakened. Someone was in our room, and I assumed they were there to steal something. I lay motionless, pretending to still be asleep. But then Evelyn yelled, "Lynda! Do you see that?"

I turned and saw nothing. But immediately I experienced something amazing. It was as if a warm breeze coming from a furnace register blew right at me. I felt paralyzed, with nothing moving but my eyes. Meanwhile, Evelyn was saying, "He's touching me!" Next, I felt the warmth intensify, and Evelyn said, "He's coming to you now!"

Suddenly, a hand was lying on my right leg just above my knee. I could feel the fingers; then after a few moments, I sensed it lift gently away as Evelyn said, "He's leaving now." And the warmth I had experienced was gone.

I ran back for the dorm mother. Her first words were, "Oh, honey, is she worse?" Without explanation, I grabbed her arm and pulled her toward our room. As I opened the door, she said, "Oh my! What's that I feel in here?" And we told her our story.

The next morning, Evelyn took her insulin, but she felt so good, she cut back on the amount. She got sick like she'd taken an overdose. She cut back more at noon, and even more that night—all with the same overdose symptoms. So the next day, she didn't take her insulin at all or the next day or the next. Three months later, at the urging of her mother, Evelyn went to the doctor. Amazed, he announced no more diabetes!

Nothing like that event ever happened to me before or since. But two truths became abundantly clear: (1) *The miraculous was truly possible*; and (2) *I could access those miracles myself because of the One I had living inside me.* Jesus made it possible by giving us the Holy

Spirit. He came to spread the good stuff around. Every work that Jesus did and even greater works (see John 14:12), we could do because the same One who raised Him from the dead dwells in you and me. Not just the pastors or evangelists or prophets. He makes His home in little ol' you and me. The Holy Spirit and His power became an equal opportunity provider. He loves inserting His power, demonstrating His goodness and answering gutsy prayers of ordinary people who ask and believe.

I wrote about this event in my freshman college English course the next year. It was our whole-quarter project. The marks my professor made in red on my narrative ended after the first couple of pages. I could almost imagine him laying down his pen and digesting what had happened to one of his students. At the top of my paper, he wrote "A Most Absorbing Narrative."

Is that how you feel? Is this the first time you've heard that the miraculous works of the Holy Spirit don't just belong to the kooky or to the famous evangelist? They're real and valid and awesome, and they can be yours and can fit right into your everyday world. My parents weren't there to pray that important prayer. They weren't there to connect heaven with earth; but this 18-year-old girl who'd come to believe the things the Holy Spirit offered—she *was* there, and she *did* make the connection. No longer was the supernatural a matter of debate or a gift that belonged only to a special few. She had learned to lean, and that made the difference in her life from then on.

You Can Do It; We Can Help

This week, I met with a woman I'll call Barb, whom I knew at a previous church I had attended where they teach that everything the Holy Spirit has to offer happens at salvation. This woman came from a very non-Christian background to become a believer in Jesus, but her husband did not follow her lead. Barb carried the sole responsibility for spiritual growth in her family, and many hardships that continued. She enthusiastically headed the women's ministry when I knew her well; but as I sat across the table from her now, five years later, I heard a weary, unvictorious, questioning woman who was about to give up on her walk of faith. And absent of going that next level with the Holy Spirit, I saw no way out for the Barb I've grown to love. We can only go so far without the enduing power of the Holy Spirit.

Barb's choice is the same as yours and mine. We can settle into comfortable, acceptable, powerless, I-hope-someone-can-do-it-for-me-when-I-need-it Christianity, or we can make our own way there. That doesn't mean we don't all need the Body of Christ to help strengthen us at times. But if we will push into the depths of everything the Holy Spirit came to bring on this side of troubles, we'll be ready and confident and equipped without intimidation when the big stuff comes along, both for ourselves and for others. If your church is doing its part, you're receiving the teaching you need for moving into the greater-works provision Jesus left for us. You're seeing the miracles and the answered prayers and learning how to do them on your own.

But if that's not happening, and you're convinced that there's a lot more empowerment that the Holy Spirit offers, you're going to have to learn it for yourself. As the coming of Jesus draws closer, troubles will grow bigger and Satan will intensify his attacks. God needs people who will be ready: those who are well acquainted with the Holy Spirit, those who will dare to stand up to the enemy, those who are armed and ready to do business and those who are experienced at achieving victory. In the quiet places of your life, you can become equipped and adept at touching heaven and getting results. Home Depot has a slogan that says, "You can do it, we can help." I'm here to remind you—you can do it—and I hope this book has helped.

Your prayer life is the place to start getting strong. How that happens is much like it was in the Old Testament tabernacle—only this time, you're the priest who has the right to enter.

In bringing yourself into God's presence, you first go into the Outer Court. You've made the effort, set aside the time, determined to do it. Your body, however, is still speaking loudly. Your mind wanders to your schedule for the day. Your tummy growls. You want to go back to sleep. But you refuse to submit to your lower nature. You resist letting your flesh be in charge and take the place of God. Something in you keeps you there as you recognize the need to crucify the flesh, deal with sin and press on into how the Holy Spirit can help you.

So you keep praying in the Spirit, and eventually you enter the Holy Place. Here your soul starts taking over. Your spiritual hunger is greater than your physical hunger. You quiet the cravings of the flesh and seek instead the cravings in you to see Him as He is. And the more time you spend in this place, the quieter the voice of your flesh grows and the louder He speaks. You sense His presence and His delight in your desire for Him. You acknowledge His reality more than ever before, and still you want more.

At last He's got you where He wants you—in the Holy of Holies—totally surrendered, completely enamored, absolutely determined. Your seeking spirit now controls your body and soul. The Christlike, completely perfect part of you called the Spirit (His Spirit in you) communes face to face with God. You can say anything to Him, and He speaks back to you. As you continue to come into this place daily, it becomes more natural more quickly. Then everything you've ever heard about Him becomes yours, really yours, and you know that out of your love for Him and His love for you, anything can happen. The greater works become normal works, a natural outgrowth of spending time with Him.

It's no more complicated than that. Out of hunger, intimacy and time spent with His Spirit, you learn to adore Him. Out of that adoration comes everything a good Father longs to give to His child. Nothing is off limits. Nothing is too big or insignificant. Everything is possible when you find that special, secret, personal, up-close place with Him. And now you can take it out *anyplace* because you've gotten to know Him *someplace. Your* place. The place that belongs to just you and Him day after day after day.

Decision Time

Crossing the Rubicon. It means to pass a point of no return, and it refers to Julius Caesar's crossing of the Rubicon River in 49 B.C.

in northeastern Italy. The crossing was considered an act of war. In today's vernacular, crossing the Rubicon means moving beyond a point where it's better to keep going than to turn back.

My guess is that you have read this book because something or Someone inside you is driving you forward. You're hungry. You're searching. You're discontent with religion as usual. You're certain there has to be more. My hope is that upon finishing this book, you will have crossed your own Rubicon, your own place of no turning back until you have achieved everything God has for you.

For some time, I've been an admirer of a couple of wonderful verses that remind me of crossing the Rubicon:

> And from the days of John the Baptist until now the king-dom of heaven suffers violence, and the violent take it by force (Matt. 11:12).

At first glance, this verse can sound like a man-only verse. Af-ter all, we women embrace our femininity. We enjoy the frills and the soft sides of our existence. We write down those 800 numbers we see advertised on TV for things that will make us *more* femi-nine, not less (things like facial hair remover and products to smooth our rough feet).

But there's another side of us women, and that's the side that makes us hardship survivors and world changers. It's the part that allows us to take on challenges—often four at a time—and succeed at them. That's why I think I can interest you in exploring what this verse can mean to you.

"Force" used here is the word *biazo,* and it means "to impose one's way into a thing." The idea here is that before John the Bap-tist, the Kingdom could only be viewed in the light of prophecy, but now it was preached! It *had* been vague, but it just got per-sonal. The Holy Spirit lit on Jesus through John as he baptized Him in the Jordan River, and you know what happened from there. The whole world was turned upside down.

People everywhere wanting a piece of this new thing crowded in with ardor resembling violence and desperation. They pursued it with abandon, and He honored their search. He gave them what He had—the Holy Spirit—and turned their relationship with God from vague to personal.

Now He seeks that kind of force, resolve, earnestness and determination in you as you move forward into the deeper, more committed, more sold-out, more deep-rooted move of the Holy Spirit—even when family and friends don't go with you and oppose you heading there too (see Matt. 10:34-39).

When you read this verse in context, you see that Jesus' references to the nonreligious style of John and the confrontational, miraculous ministry of Elijah teach that the kingdom of God makes its penetration by a kind of violent entry opposing the human status quo (see Matt. 11:8-19). He wasn't doing things like they'd always been done. His wasn't a take-it-or-leave it, sometimes-on-and-sometimes-off commitment. His ministry transcended the "softness" (see v. 8) of staid religious formalism and exceeded the pretension of child's play (see vv. 16-17). It refused to "dance to the music" of society's expectation that the religious community provide either entertainment ("we played the flute") or dead traditionalism ("we mourned").

Jesus defines the "violence" of His kingdom's expansion by defining the "sword" and "fire" He brought. It was different from the battle techniques of political provocation or armed advance. It is the result of God's order shaking relationships, households, cities and nations by the entry of the Holy Spirit's power working in everyone willing to take the journey with Him. It's called radical abandonment. Now look at this companion verse:

> The law and the prophets were until John. Since that time the kingdom of God has been preached, and everyone is pressing into it (Luke 16:16).

"Pressing into it." What dynamic words! Jesus is reminding us that the gospel of the Kingdom must be accompanied with spiritual passion; otherwise passivity takes over. Pressing in—even if you're going it alone—is accomplished first through prayer coupled with a will to surrender one's life and self-interests to the ministry of the Holy Spirit.

Moses made sure God was going with him as he crossed his Rubicon. In Exodus 33:15-16, he told God, "If Your Presence does not go with us, do not bring us up from here. For how then will it be known that Your people and I have found grace in your sight, except You go with us?" You're not crossing your Rubicon alone, either. You're partnering with the Holy Spirit, and along with Him come the other two, God the Father and God the Son. You get it all, just by following the lead of the Holy Spirit.

No More *Tohu* and *Bohu*

How glorious to realize where we've come from, where we are and where we're going. In the beginning, "The earth was without form [*tohu*], and void [*bohu*]" (Gen. 1:2). *Tohu* and *bohu*—those words just about say it all (and they're funny at that!). It was a scene of disorder, confusion, formlessness, chaos, worthlessness, emptiness, desolation and lack of arrangement. But God had things under control. He looked down at the scene of chaos and saw order, strength and balance.

> Declaring the end from the beginning, and from ancient times things that are not yet done, saying, "My counsel shall stand, and I will do all My pleasure" (Isa. 46:10).

> I have declared the former things from the beginning; they went forth from My mouth, and I caused them to hear it. Suddenly I did them, and they came to pass (Isa. 48:3).

In this last verse, the word translated "suddenly" is the Greek word *idou* and the Hebrew word *pith'owm*. It means "whoosh!" Isn't that great? God purposed something in His mind and spoke it from His mouth. Even though time elapsed, *whoosh*, the inevitable happened at just the right moment when the Holy Spirit brought it about. Then we have Jesus speaking before He was ever born about His role in the Trinity, and what He had to offer you and me:

Come near to Me, hear this: I have not spoken in secret from the beginning; from the time that it was, I was there. And now the Lord GOD and His Spirit have sent Me (Isa. 48:16).

Your life once reflected only *tohu* and *bohu.* But God had it under control. His Spirit wooed you until, *whoosh,* what God planned happened. You trusted in Jesus as your Lord and the Holy Spirit moved in. But He wasn't finished. He kept after you. He wouldn't let you stay where you were. He urged, prodded and made you hunger for more. He engineered circumstances and brought people (and yes, even books) around you to encourage your search.

And now *whoosh!* What He has drawn you toward is about to happen. You're learning to lean on your own and are finding more power than you ever dreamed. Now, just wait! You can't even believe where He's going to take you from here.

Different Paths

The first winter we lived in Colorado, I took my kids skiing. They had learned on bumps in Ohio, and the first place I exposed them to was Copper Mountain, which offers ski runs above 12,000 feet.

Needless to say, it was somewhat of a shock to my children, especially to eight-year-old Clint. I got off the chairlift with Ashley and Clint. She couldn't wait to get going, and he couldn't wait to go home. Clint said, "I'm not going down there!"

I sent Ashley ahead to the closest chair lift below, and Clint and I began our careful descent. On the way down, I *encouraged* him by telling him he had what it took. I *modeled* for him by showing him how to snowplow down the slope. I *protected* him from the speedy snowboarders flying down from behind. I *guided* him by showing him which paths to take.

As soon as the chairlift was in sight where we would meet Ashley, Clint skied past me saying, "Come on, Mom. Can't you go any faster?" I watched as he made his own tracks and took his own path different from mine. Suddenly, I realized I'd just witnessed a summary of my role as his mom: encouraging, modeling, protecting, guiding and then letting him go.

And now I realize it just might represent a summary of my role with you too. I've encouraged you to step out and get to know the Holy Spirit in a deeper way. I've modeled some of the successful ways I have seen this happen in my own life. I've protected you from some of the pitfalls in your search. I've guided you in effective ways for getting it done.

But ultimately, I recognize that your growing relationship with the Holy Spirit will take you down different paths than my own. The plans He has for you are not the same as the ones He has had for me. Your generation can go further than mine. Your participation in the miraculous can be bigger than anything I ever imagined.

If even in a small way you've realized that *you* can do it, and *I* helped, I will have accomplished my goal. I will have assisted you in making the Holy Spirit and everything He has to offer you at home in your heart. I will have taken one more step toward fulfilling my life purpose. And what a privilege it has been!

The grace of the Lord Jesus Christ, and the love of God, and the communion of the Holy Spirit be with you all. Amen (2 Cor. 13:14).

Make It Yours
Make Him at Home in Your Heart

What you're considering—crossing over, going deeper, pressing in, taking by force everything God has for you—is no small commitment. It's also not to be taken lightly. The Bible tells us to count the cost before beginning new things for Him (see Luke 14:28). It would be good to stop right now and write out a goal and cost analysis for what you are wanting to do. How about doing that with me?

_____

_____

_____

_____

What do you want to change in your relationship with the Holy Spirit?

_____

_____

_____

_____

What will that change involve?

_____

_____

_____

_____

What challenges might you face?

_____

_____

_____

Who will be affected?

_____

_____

_____

_____

What sacrifices will you need to make?

_____

_____

_____

_____

Are you willing to do what it takes to accomplish your goal? How
do you know?

_____

_____

_____

Sometimes the quickest way to build your own faith is to help
build the faith of someone else. Read the following two Bible stories, and then answer the questions below.

> Jesus went up to Jerusalem. Now there is in Jerusalem by
> the Sheep Gate a pool, which is called in Hebrew,
> Bethesda, having five porches. In these lay a great multi-
> tude of sick people, blind, lame, paralyzed, waiting for the
> moving of the water. For an angel went down at a certain
> time into the pool and stirred up the water; then whoever
> stepped in first, after the stirring of the water, was made
> well of whatever disease he had. Now a certain man was
> there who had an infirmity thirty-eight years. When Jesus
> saw him lying there, and knew that he already had been in
> that condition a long time, He said to him, "Do you want
> to be made well?" The sick man answered Him, "Sir, I have
> no man to put me into the pool when the water is stirred
> up; but while I am coming, another steps down before
> me." Jesus said to him, "Rise, take up your bed and walk."
> And immediately the man was made well, took up his bed,
> and walked (John 5:1-18).

> And again He entered Capernaum after some days, and it
> was heard that He was in the house. Immediately many
> gathered together, so that there was no longer room to re-
> ceive them, not even near the door. And He preached the
> word to them. Then they came to Him, bringing a para-
> lytic who was carried by four men. And when they could
> not come near Him because of the crowd, they uncovered
> the roof where He was. So when they had broken through,

they let down the bed on which the paralytic was lying. When Jesus saw their faith, He said to the paralytic, "Son, your sins are forgiven you." And some of the scribes were sitting there and reasoning in their hearts, "Why does this Man speak blasphemies like this? Who can forgive sins but God alone?" But immediately, when Jesus perceived in His spirit that they reasoned thus within themselves, He said to them, "Why do you reason about these things in your hearts? Which is easier, to say to the paralytic, 'Your sins are forgiven you,' or to say, 'Arise, take up your bed and walk'? But that you may know that the Son of Man has power on earth to forgive sins"—He said to the paralytic, "I say to you, arise, take up your bed, and go to your house." Immediately he arose, took up the bed, and went out in the presence of them all, so that all were amazed and glorified God, saying, "We never saw anything like this!" (Mark 2:1-12).

What do these two stories tell you about how these guys realized they had what it took to get the job done?

_____

_____

_____

_____

What do these two stories tell you about the lengths to which you should go to access miracles for someone else?

_____

_____

_____

_____

How did they capitalize on *dunamis* power and *exousia* authority?

_____

_____

_____

What evidence of *parrhesia* boldness did you see on the behalf of someone else?

_____

_____

_____

_____

What person comes to mind that you need to aid in bringing about their miracle?

_____

_____

_____

_____

As you close the cover of this book, what new chapter are you opening in your life? Describe it thoroughly, and then write your prayer confession below, summarizing where you intend to go.

_____

_____

_____

_____

PRAYER CONFESSION

Holy Spirit,

_____

_____

_____

_____

_____

Amen and Amen.

Note

1. John Stallings, "Learning to Lean," © 1976 HeartWarming Music/BMI.

Created for Purpose Ministries
with Lynda Hunter Bjorklund, Ed.D.

www.CreatedForPurpose.com

Dedicated to equipping women with everyday wisdom
for fulfilling their ultimate calling.

Please visit the site for a FREE offer. Stay connected
with Lynda and her ministry on:

Facebook
Twitter
YouTube
LinkedIN

You can contact Lynda for a speaking engagement at:
LyndaBjorklund@CreatedForPurpose.com